A BODY BROKEN,
A BODY BETRAYED

A BODY BROKEN, A BODY BETRAYED

RACE, MEMORY, AND EUCHARIST
IN WHITE-DOMINANT CHURCHES

Mary McClintock Fulkerson
and Marcia W. Mount Shoop

CASCADE *Books* • Eugene, Oregon

A BODY BROKEN, A BODY BETRAYED
Race, Memory, and Eucharist in White-Dominated Churches

Cascade Books
An Imprint of Wipf and Stock Publishers
199 W. 8th Ave., Suite 3
Eugene, OR 97401

www.wipfandstock.com

ISBN 13: 978-1-62032-904-7

Cataloging-in-Publication data:

Fulkerson, Mary McClintock, 1950–

   A body broken, a body betrayed : race, memory, and eucharist in white-dominant churches / Mary McClintock Fulkerson and Marcia W. Mount Shoop.

   xvi + 90 p. ; 21.5 cm. —Includes bibliographical references.

   ISBN 13: 978-1-62032-904-7

   1. Lord's Supper and Christian union. 2. Race relations—Religious aspects—Christianity. I. Mount Shoop, Marcia W. II. Title.

BT702 .F85 2015

Manufactured in the U.S.A.

Dedicated to
the great cloud of witnesses who have gathered at the Table
across the world and through the ages

If you know these things, you are blessed if you do them.

—THE GOSPEL OF JOHN 13:17

Contents

Preface

As a white woman raised and ordained in the Presbyterian Church (U.S.A.), I grew up in a predominantly white Protestant denomination. Even as schools have gradually become more racially diverse, my childhood experience growing up in the 1950s and 1960s in the South was very segregated. My "religious" experience in Presbyterian churches was pretty much the same. Language of "loving thy neighbor" and "welcoming all of God's children" was common but rarely, if ever, embodied so that "neighbor" intentionally invoked racial and class diversity.

What has been challenging and transformative for my habituation into being part of the dominant race and class began as an academic exploration of the dynamics of an interracial church. The community I studied was primarily comprised of African American and white folks, as well as persons with disabilities. I discovered that despite my theoretical commitment to welcoming the "other," my experiential and bodily habituation was deeply shaped by "white ownership of space," as one of my African American colleagues defines it.

Being a minority was a difficult but crucial transitional experience. My pursuit of this project exploring white practices of colorblind racism became a possibility after that research, but has been particularly enhanced by my friendship with Marcia, whose awareness and work around racial diversity in the PC (U.S.A.) were and continue to be profoundly rich and generative. Our work together has been quite important for me, and my primary acknowledgments must be of the community I "studied" and continue to

ix

participate in and of Marcia, whose deep wisdom about church and white colorblindness made this book possible.

I am also grateful to William Hart, who gave me language for my colorblindness. I continue to be thankful for Leoneda Inge, who co-leads the Pauli Murray reading group with me at our multiracial church, as well as those church members who have shared stories about their own experience of race throughout our five years of gathering monthly to explore and celebrate the life of the famous activist and lesbian who was the first female African American to be ordained as an Episcopal priest. And there are of course so many others whose lives and wisdom have mattered so much to me, even if I cannot name them all here.

Mary McClintock Fulkerson
Durham, North Carolina

‿

Like Mary, I grew up steeped in the culture of the Presbyterian Church (U.S.A.). Even with a "racism-aware" household, a father who was a card-carrying member of the NAACP, and a mother from southern Mississippi with stories of antiracist activism in her family at a time and in a place where white people just didn't do such things, I did not begin to understand how deeply the dynamics of whiteness had shaped me until I was an adult. Going deeper than commitments to racial justice can be excruciating for white people, maybe especially for white people like me who wanted to believe we are different, we are "good" white people. Going deeper, however, has been a life-giving practice that keeps me on a healing path around the wounds of race and privilege.

There have been and continue to be many steps along the way in this journey with race and privilege in my life, but the most profound aspect is a very personal and precious one that words will always fail to describe adequately. That radical shift has come through love—the love my husband, John, and I have for our godson, Chris. Chris Dixon came into our lives almost twenty years ago as an eleven-year-old growing up across the street from the church we attended in Charlotte, North Carolina. What started out as a pretty typical white, justice-oriented act of helping someone in need quickly became a connection that changed everything for us. In helping to parent Chris all of these years, I have learned more about my whiteness than from anything else in my life. These years of life together have been complicated and joyful, heartbreaking and heart-making. The love of this relationship and the growth of seeing myself and Chris in new ways are etched into this book.

I have also been blessed beyond measure by my colleagues, my sisters and brothers in Christ, whom I have worked alongside in the multicultural[1] movement in the Presbyterian Church (U.S.A.) and in ecumenical circles with others who are hungry for a church that embodies God's complexity with more integrity. There is no way I can name everyone in this Spirit-filled movement who has blessed my life. The Rev. James Lee, the Rev. Raafat Girgis, the Rev. Magdalena Garcia, the Rev. Dr. Wanda Lundy, the Rev. Dr. Gun Ho Lee, the Rev. Jerrod Lowry, the Rev. Nibs Stroupe, and the Rev. Jake Kim are just a few of the people from the Presbyterian context who have been a blessing on this journey.

I have appreciated the work of Mary McClintock Fulkerson for a long time. I give thanks for the opportunity to build a friendship with her during my family's time in Chapel Hill, North Carolina. Mary and I immediately found that we had a shared passion for the exploration of race and privilege. For both of us this passion comes from the heart of our lives as believers and as theologians. This passion comes fraught with pain and disappointment. It also comes with deep conviction. Mary's diligence and intellect have made this project more conversant with a broader set of questions. She is forever finding more resources, more conversation partners, and more insights. I am grateful for the texture

---

1. Part of our growth as a movement includes how we name and identify ourselves. The word *multicultural* is not without problems. I tend to use *cross-cultural* and *inter-cultural* more frequently now, but the movement itself is still most often recognized by the word *multicultural*.

those commitments brought to this book. And I am also grateful that our friendship continues from here.

I also extend my gratitude to all the church communities who have helped form me and who have welcomed me into their midst as pastor, teacher, preacher, officiant at the Lord's Table, and child of God. This book is written for the church and toward the redemptive promise that we profess. Thanks be to God for the visions that call us toward healing the Body of Christ.

Marcia W. Mount Shoop
West Lafayette, Indiana

Prolegomenon

Bodies matter
Christ's body, broken for you and me
Our bodies, broken and born
into layers of ambiguity and promise

Bodies are not independent, discrete, cut off
We are enfleshed and entangled with all that is
The blood that flows through our spidering veins
Is the water that laps the shores of lakefronts and oceansides

Bodies are never-not tangled up with shared oxygen
and with the telltale signs of our distortion, toxins
and the sharp edges of quiet violence
that draw themselves especially toward the
biases of pigment, genitalia, and other accidents of birth

These bodies feed on connection
They languish in isolation
And they simultaneously inherit and create worlds
Unique and shared, brutal and promising

Primal, cellular, flesh navigation
That is how we live and move and have our being
There is no body apart from some body
And there is no some body apart from
other bodies—otherized bodies, racialized bodies,
gendered bodies, sacralized bodies,
wounded and healing bodies

We share One body
Multifarious emergence
Irreducible particularities
Identities taught, fraught, sought, and
Processing from hard truths and dreams
That we can taste and see
And hunger for all the more

Bodies matter
And they gather
They notice hunger
Unless they have gone too long without
Being fed

Bodies matter
And we wonder
How it is that we are invited to live
And breathe lives
that matter, too

And His body, the body
who reverberates our distortion
And our redemption
Betrayal and regeneration
The body that scoffs at death and
Defines new birth

His body traveled through a birth canal
And fingered wounds—his and ours
He had eyes to see
And he tasted
our pain and promise

He took bread and ripped it
Into pieces that might feed us
Our bodies, not simply our imagination
But the cells that divide
connect, create, perish, and live

Marcia W. Mount Shoop, 2014

one

Race, Memory, and Eucharist:
An Introduction

Our stories tell us who we are, at least that is what Christianity tells us. Our salvation story, the stories of Scripture, and testimonies of faith define us and inform our religious identities. But what about when our stories are incomplete? Or worse yet, what about when our stories about ourselves are lies? What about when stories dis-member or contort part of the Body of Christ by denying truth, silencing dissonance, or ignoring wounds?

The communion table is set for us as a place where we come to be welcomed and reconciled to God. Scripture tells us that in God's kingdom people from all nations, from all tribes and tongues will come to stand before the throne of God, singing praises (Rev 7:9). Jesus called himself the bread of life (John 6:48) and the true vine (John 15:1). Scripture tells us about Christ's last supper with his friends in an upstairs room. There he called the bread they ate his body, he told them the wine was the new covenant sealed in his blood, and he told them to eat it and drink it all (Luke 22). There he named the betrayal that would condemn him to death: "But see, the one who betrays me is with me, and his hand is on the table" (Luke 22:21); there he told the truth about the friends who would harm him: "You will all become deserters because of me this night" (Matt 26:31; Mark 14:27). And "troubled in spirit," he declared after washing his disciples' feet that "one of you will betray me"

(John 14:21). And Scripture tells us this is a meal that, whenever celebrated, is to be done in remembrance of him (1 Cor 11:23–26).

And our institutional memory sifts through these stories to further interpret what happens at Eucharist and how it is achieved. John Calvin articulated the Reformed formula that the mystery and power of the Holy Spirit assure us of the real presence of Christ in our communion meal, "as if Christ were placed in bodily presence before our view, or handled by our hands."[1] Calvin describes how we are nourished at the Table with words like "refresh, strengthen, and exhilarate." Calvin basked in the mysterious efficacy of Eucharist, by the power of the Holy Spirit, to "truly unite things separated by space."[2] Somehow Christ dwells in us; somehow we, as gathered communities of disparate believers, are transformed into his body in the world.

Eucharistic liturgy and habit cultivate the expectation that we have a shared story and that we embody this shared story in our eucharistic practice. Yet when real bodies gather at the table there is a thoroughgoing dissonance that signals rupture and betrayal as well as particularity and possibility. Estranged relationships are allowed to splinter, and instead of seeing all nations and tongues represented at the table, often we look around and see people just like us. And many quietly partake of this feast we're told reflects God's hopes for humankind even as we are left thirsty and hungry for true communities of difference and reconciliation. We nibble at the bread of life and sip the cup of salvation. We keep our eyes down, wondering if we should taste more. With the echoes of an invitation to come and encounter the Body of Christ lingering in the air, we sit and wait for another day's sensation.

For most Christians the failure to duplicate Jesus' healing meals with outsiders is not intentional. Most churches understand themselves to be welcoming communities. "Inclusiveness" is a frequent descriptor in many church mission statements. Indeed, white-dominant churches have exorcised themselves of one of our nation's most egregious forms of exclusion—the historic sin

1. Calvin, *Institutes*, Book IV, 558.
2. Ibid., 563.

2

of racial segregation. Like most white Americans, predominantly white churches claim to be "colorblind." That is, many predominantly white churches aspire to see all persons, regardless of color, as God's children.[3]

A dominant contemporary white narrative is that of the church as a welcoming, colorblind community that gathers at the Table regularly to be reconciled with God as members somehow encounter the body and blood of Christ. The Eucharist is often equated with the social witness of the church: "Liturgy *is social* action,"[4] says Stanley Hauerwas, and Bernd Wannewetsch asserts that "it is *in worship itself* that the ethical in-forming of human acting and judging comes about."[5] If this is so, what kind of "social action" is being narrated and performed by this purportedly welcoming colorblind table fellowship? Despite the well-meaning discourse, this is a narrative and practice in dominant populations that bears more scrutiny, especially if we take Calvin seriously that in communion it is "as if Christ were placed in bodily presence before our view, or handled by our hands."[6] If Christ's presence has to do with bodies—his, of course, and ours as the "Body of Christ"—then the bodies at the Table matter.

To understand the function of Eucharist both in reproducing social brokenness and in potentially aiding in the transformation of our brokenness, we need a framework wise to the complexity of social trauma, race, and embodiment. We need more than the traditional visions of the past, whether that of Luther or of Calvin, of

3. There have been and continue to be differences between African American churches and predominantly white churches with regard to such postures. For an important study of different liturgical practices and worldviews relative to racial difference, see Haldeman, *Towards Liturgies That Reconcile.*

4. Hauerwas, *Christian Existence Today,* 107.

5. According to Wannenwetsch, "The formative happening takes place in the context of a human *receptivity which can also be described as acting and judging.* So the acting and judging of beings is only an outgrowth of worship, a possibility which *then* arises of responding in daily life to the acting and judging of God which has been experienced. It is *in worship itself* that the ethical in-forming of human acting and judging comes about." *Political Worship,* 6.

6. Calvin, *Institutes,* Book IV, 558

the early church or of medieval liturgy.[7] We need greater attention to the connections between embodied practice and theological imagination.[8] To identify and better address the "colorblindness" associated with much liturgical bodily practice, it is important to identify the nature of the problem as defined by bodies, social memory, and the ways that racialized injustices continue to impact our lives.[9] These patterns and practices embody the marks of traumatic memory in the unruly ways racialized violence (both systemic and chronic) reiterates itself in trivialized practices and mentalities. We invite a re-membering of Eucharist both by interrogating colorblindness and by making space for acknowledging the traumatic imprint of race in our believing communities. These focal points allow us to point toward transformative capacity in the way we re-member our Eucharistic practice.

Embodied Re-membering:
Social Trauma and Racialized Communities

The word *trauma* literally means "wound." In Greek it refers to a wound of the body. Its contemporary use expands *trauma* to refer to "collective suffering," a suffering given further nuance relative to different theorizations of trauma.[10] Freudian theories around trauma shifted the focus on trauma's wounds toward the mind.[11]

---

7. Haldeman argues that liturgical theology "typically has two tendencies: to be critical of a contemporary practice and to be nostalgic as a way to address the problem." Even the standard ordo desired by many forms of liturgical scholarship, he argues, is not adequate to "fix" contemporary liturgical problems. Haldeman, *Toward Liturgies That Reconcile*, 3.

8. Liturgical scholar Siobhán Garrigan would agree. In her book on ritual she argues for attention to the face-to-face or intersubjective relations of Eucharist and its performativity. See Garrigan, *Beyond Ritual*.

9. Haldeman's work on the liturgical differences between African American worship and white Protestant worship also offers a fascinating study of different models for interracial worship that is not blind to the typical dominance of white practices. See his *Toward Liturgies That Reconcile*.

10. Alexander, *Trauma*, 2

11. Caruth, *Unclaimed Experience*, 3–4.

Many contemporary trauma theories are informed by Freud's understanding that the mind is not able to take in the immediate force of trauma and also by developing understandings of how bodies hold trauma. Trauma is, therefore, not fully integrated into consciousness but "imposes itself again, repeatedly" in nightmares, in repetitive actions, and in habituations.[12] Trauma is characterized by this simultaneity of deeply embodied impact and unassimilated experience. Cathy Caruth describes the dynamic of trauma as "complex ways of knowing and not knowing." The wounds of trauma "cry out" in the attempt to tell us of a reality or truth that is not otherwise available.[13]

The continued reality of trauma extends onto the larger template of history itself. History "bears the marks of trauma" in its endless repetition of violence.[14] Such endurance also requires the emergence of ongoing cultural representation and structural support. Indeed, the actual public awareness of a group's social suffering depends upon the successful distribution of these cultural representations and systems of support.[15] Representation is key to whether a collective harm or trauma is recognized, how it is recognized or defined, and the degree to which wider audiences take responsibility.[16] The "carrier group," that is, those who are marked by racism and who try to communicate the nature of the harm and attribution of responsibility, have always had narratives of horrific oppression and lament over the centuries, "counter-memories" to the dominant ones.[17] However, their access to modes of communication and to the power to persuade the larger population was

---

12. Ibid., 4.

13. Ibid.

14. Lange, *Trauma Recalled*, 99.

15. Alexander, *Trauma*, 15–30.

16. According to Jeffrey Alexander's social theory of trauma.

17. Ron Eyerman says that African Americans produced a "counter-memory," a term he borrows from Foucault. He provides a helpful complexification of this topic, pointing out that while it has been "always there as a referent" for different generations, there has never been one African American narrative of slavery. Eyerman, *Cultural Trauma*, 7, 18, 10–21.

of course profoundly constrained in the days of slavery.[18] Despite improvement over time, the concealment of this social harm is complex and ongoing. Given the complexities of trauma, the history of race in American religious communities unfolds and conceals itself in ways that we cannot fully describe or control but that are deeply formative.

Tangled in this snarl of dissonance, trivialization, estrangement, rhetoric, and possibility are tenacious threads of white denial and obliviousness. Race in white contexts is often cast as an issue that surfaces only when people of color bring it up—otherwise, everything is "fine." And many whites tend to navigate the world with the "I'm not a racist" mantra, all the while embodying unconscious racialized assumptions and biases that help form everything from neighborhoods to public and private policies, from gut reactions to people of color to intimate relationships. Privilege becomes obscured and affirmed by means of stories of the whence and the why of who we are and where we've been. Troubled, trivialized, and tormented memories conspire to render all the more tenacious the mentalities and blind spots of institutions like the church.

And even as many whites and the institutions they have historically controlled engage in storytelling and work that is aimed at liberation, the realities of the layers and layers of habituation that tell the embodied stories of racialized harm may be used to blame and judge those who have been most deeply harmed. These signs of ravaged generations become ways to justify continued cultural estrangement and even white mystification around the whence of many of our society's social challenges. This white denial is both stealthy and tenacious and bears itself out in a staggering amount of data about how whites tend to understand the status of equity and fairness in the United States.

18. Alexander, *Trauma*, 15–30. The full list of themes in the master narrative includes identifying the nature of pain, the nature of victims, the relation of victims to wider audiences, and attribution of responsibility.

Most whites assume that systems in this country are accessible and fair to people of all races.[19] Even whites who may have a more critical awareness of things like higher conviction rates for people of color in our judicial system, higher rates of poverty for people of color, and "achievement gap" data often have trouble understanding how to connect these dynamics to racism, and in particular to white privilege. All the while, racism and white privilege continue to erode and diminish communities, relationships, and possibilities for change. The effects of racism permeate everything from the rates of disease and infant mortality (even when data takes into account economic and education levels), to wealth, to financing and housing patterns, to the differences in frequency and method of discipline used with white schoolkids and those of color, to patterns of incarceration, to the ways we embody faith practices.[20]

The wounds of racism are and have been experienced quite consciously as trauma by people of color even as they continue to have profound unconscious and embodied effects. The necessary function of cultural representation and structures to foreground and define the trauma surfaces here, especially as the public representation of this collective suffering has changed over the years.[21] We can trace these changes from explicit denial in white narratives justifying slavery, to the framing of racial trauma via civil rights discourse, to the more recent narrative of colorblindness. The "not-knowing" that attends trauma takes hold in unique and particular ways and is, therefore, also profoundly shaped by cultural context.

19. Tim Wise's book *Colorblind* outlines many studies that indicate these patterns of white denial. See in particular chapter 2, "The Trouble with Post-racial Liberalism."

20. Wise outlines several sources of data around all of these issues (except the ecclesial dynamics). His section titled "Racism, Discrimination, and Health Care" provides an overwhelming amount of information about the deep and persistent effects of racism on black and brown populations. He writes, "In the past several years more than a hundred studies have found a relationship between racial discrimination and negative physical health outcomes for people of color." Wise, *Colorblind*, 112–26, 116.

21. Alexander, *Trauma*, 6.

Some social groups may have, for example, repressed certain experiences of violence, and some, as Alexander points out, "can, and often do, refuse to recognize the existence of others' trauma, or place the responsibility for it on people other than themselves."[22]

Historical acknowledgment of complicity in injustice by dominant groups is a fundamental step toward progress. William Bridges' diagram for the process of successful transition through social trauma maps out collective naming and recognition as essential to constructive change.[23] However, commonly heard claims such as "I didn't own slaves" and "segregation is illegal now" illustrate the view that "the problem is over—let's move on," and can function as modes of avoidance and denial. It is precisely this avoidance and denial that help *prevent* the process of collective transition through social trauma. Continued residuals of this trauma are also found in white bodily habituations toward that "other" social group. Such aversive bodily habituations can sometimes display this preconscious avoidance while those who are racialized may embody habits of survival because of the dynamics of marginalization and the stress of constantly encountering white biases and white-defined systems. And these traumatic and re-traumatizing patterns can stitch themselves into and through cultures because of their shared legacy.

The colorblind narrative around the Lord's Table embodies this social "not-knowing" that continues to mask the ongoing effects of the wounds of racism. Traumatic repetition and return play out in relationships ruptured by a violent past that visits and revisits itself upon us without our bidding, even against our will. The full force of these wounds comes not in a story long past but in a present captive to habits, patterns, and denial of the traumatic truth itself.

For us, Eucharist also provides a template through which we can see ourselves and the marks of racialized trauma more clearly. And Eucharist is a mechanism that creates space for new reenactments that could integrate traumatic repetition and embodied

22. Ibid.

23. Dukes et al., "Collective Transitions," 231–52.

practices with life-giving possibilities. Eucharist tells us who we are, even as it calls us to who God hopes we can be. It is the dissonance between the stories we tell around the Table and the practices we embody at that same Table that creates the conditions of possibility for a new healing awareness of what have been our unconscious distortions. The wound of race surfaces at the Lord's Table and calls out for acknowledgment and transformation.

A Dominant Narrative: Welcoming, Colorblind Society

A popular narrative of many Americans is the view that we have resolved the injustices of racism. We are a "colorblind" society. "I don't see color; I just see people," the saying goes. This popular narrative of colorblindness, however, has not effected much change in the social, material, and embodied realities of race relations in the United States. Income, education, and access to privilege are still significantly differentiated by race. As many sociologists insist, this white habit of colorblindness tends to assume that racism is an individual, intentional act; racism has thus been addressed because most of us are "well-meaning," not members of the Ku Klux Klan. The prominence of the colorblind mantra is a clear example that the carrier group—those most harmed by the trauma of racism—does not yet have enough power to define the master narrative for the larger society.

When it comes to residual, structural racism, this colorblind narrative about the country, while well-intentioned, is a fiction.[24] Because this story and the habits that accompany it assume that antisegregation and other equal rights legislation fixed our problems around racism, most whites are able to ignore the structural/institutional complexities of racism that still exist. Many whites may be well-intentioned and even justice-minded, but the formation of individual and collective social consciousness still needs moral categories that acknowledge the depth and complexity of

24. See Kinder and Sears, "Prejudice and Politics," 414–31; Carr, "Color-Blind" Racism; Bonilla-Silva, Racism without Racists; Bonilla-Silva, White Supremacy.

agency that race and privilege require.[25] Sociologist Eduardo Bonilla-Silva describes most white narratives about race relations as illustrative of "color-blind racism."[26]

Colorblindness is thus not simply an intellectual conviction or belief. If it did have causal force as a conviction, especially given how widely held it is, the inclusive and implicitly welcoming tenor of the theme "colorblindness" should play out in a significant increase in white "interaction with minorities in general and blacks in particular," says Bonilla-Silva. However, his study of white patterns of interracial interactions has yielded a very different result. Instead of a welcoming set of interracial lived practices, Bonilla-Silva found a prominent "white habitus," characterized by "a set of primary networks and associations with other whites that reinforces the racial order by fostering racial solidarity among whites and negative affect toward racial 'others.'"[27]

Further categorization of these wounds is found in applied behavioral science research, which challenges the "outdated notion" that "prejudice" can be defined as explicit bias. Tim Wise describes this colorblindness among white progressives as "post-racial liberalism."[28] Rather, the effect of prejudicial stereotyping on our behavior "does not require personal animus, hostility, or even awareness" because the predominant mode of prejudice is "implicit," that is, "unwitting, unintentional and uncontrollable— even among the most well-intentioned people." Furthermore, implicit prejudice dominates; it is "ubiquitous."[29] Indeed, research has shown that most whites who claim "egalitarian values and

---

25. Of the many authors who explore this colorblindness, one very compelling example is found in Joe Feagin and Eileen O'Brien's accounts of white male executives' discourse on race. See Feagin and O'Brien, *White Men on Race*, especially the chapter titled "The White Bubble," 30–65.

26. Bonilla-Silva, *Racism without Racists*. Bonilla-Silva is not the only one who uses this term. See also Feagin and O'Brien, *White Men on Race*, 17; Hacker, *Two Nations*, 52.

27. Bonilla-Silva, *Racism without Racists*, 16.

28. Wise, *Colorblind*.

29. Hardin and Banaji, "Nature of Implicit Prejudice," 13–31.

non-prejudiced attitudes also . . . harbor unconscious negative feelings and beliefs about African Americans."[30]

While primary identification with one's own group (accompanied by the view that others are outsiders of some sort) is not a surprising human characteristic, applied behavioral science research confirms a deeply problematic role for implicit *racial* bias in our society. Even as implicit bias toward other groups can be found in all humans, its social *impact* has much to do with the *power and status* of one's group. Such bias is deeply formed by cultural stereotypes and the resulting social categorization that stigmatizes the "others." Deeply entrenched negative biases toward black and brown bodies in our society continue to exist, in part "because of basic principles associated with categorization that promote bias" and, clearly, the power to produce and spread these categories.[31] Thus, while the narrative of "colorblindness" may be unintentionally and subtly racist, it has negative impacts.

White eucharistic habits may well perform this American narrative. While our sacramental gatherings as the Body of Christ are framed with Jesus' story and other biblical narratives, in mainline denominational churches the other bodies at the Table are overwhelmingly white. The percentage of significantly interracial churches—communities in which no more than 80 percent of the membership identifies as the same race—is amazingly low: only 7 percent of American congregations qualify.[32] Thus Haldeman

30. Shelton et al., "Biases in Interracial Interactions," 32–51.

31. Ibid, 34. Well-meaning mantras do not necessarily correlate with altered social connections. Antiracism activist and author Tim Wise explores the effect of these colorblind mentalities and habits on contemporary American political culture. He points to myths such as racial transcendence (buoyed by things like President Obama's election) that snuff out public discourse about the lasting effects of racism in favor of more palatable "post-racial" rhetoric around poverty that applies to and benefits everyone, not just people of color. This "post-racial" rhetoric retains an ethic of social action even as it denies the deep and lasting effects of racism's wounds.

32. Michael Emerson, e-mail communication, October 23, 2001. See his important work with fellow sociologist Christian Smith on the role of religion in the racialization of the U.S. in Emerson, *Divided by Faith*, 10. Data collected by the Pew Forum on Religion and Public Life in a survey conducted in

asserts, "In regard to the race issue in the US, Christian worship has served most often to divide and oppress rather than to unite and liberate."[33] The invoking of welcome and inclusion in the Body of Christ in far too many churches would appear to be simply a rhetorical gesture toward differently racialized "others" by those with the assumed and illusory privilege of not having "race," that is, of being white.[34] Narrating this white-defined Table as a place where all of God's people from all nations, all tongues come to sing God's praises dis-members a past that has yet to be re-membered.

Eucharistic Re-membering and Traumatic Memory

What bodies actually gather around the Table coupled with the sacramental rhetoric of reconciliation and redemption reveals a dis-membered Body of Christ. Like a phantom limb that leaves residues of sensation, we can inhabit a space of denial around the Table even as the bodies there reenact a habit of dis-membered community and connection. We gather as a contorted, truncated, dis-membered Body.[35] What separates us is a quiet violence tenaciously continuing to rupture those whom God hopes can be together.

Dirk Lange connects Eucharist to traumatic memory through the event that we remember and ritualize in the sacrament, the Christ event. For Lange it is not the previous violence of crucifixion

---

2009 finds the following stats on racial makeup of Christian churches, where "white" does not include Hispanics: mainline Protestant churches are 91 percent white; Evangelical Protestant churches are 81 percent white; Catholic churches are 65 percent white; and Orthodox churches are 87 percent white. Cited in Robinson, *Race and Theology,* 81.

33. Haldeman, *Towards Liturgies That Reconcile,* 4.

34. Sociologist Korie Edwards' study of interracial churches found that even in communities with differently racialized bodies at the table, whites tended to dominate. Edwards, *The Elusive Dream.*

35. The nature of "dismemberment" embodies widely variant dynamics in our highly racialized culture. For instance, the power dynamics and liberative capacities of an all-black congregation gathered around the communion table carry a different quality and possibility than an all-white congregation might.

itself that is repeated around the table but the inaccessibility of the event. "The Christ event returns as a force that continually disrupts our usual forms of remembering and ritualizing."[36] Lange describes the repetition enacted in the Eucharist as "iteration" which is "continually failed remembering."[37]

Knit through this impossible memory of Christ's presence are all the strands of violence that we inherit and enact in our communal re-membering. The impossibility seeps into and through the palpable deficiencies and pain. The fragments of untold and untellable marks of racial violence add layers of impossibility to this already inaccessible memory. How we know and what we can know swirls in and through rote rehearsal of a story we are not sure we know how to make our own. These shards and fragments, these repetitions and rehearsals, and these dis-membered and re-membered bodies coalesce around a Table where we hear of a body broken and of blood spilled for us.

Re-membering a dis-membered Body acquaints us with the shadows of the violence done to that Body. Re-membering violence, re-membering rupture and fissure and harm, is traumatic memory. The fragmented memory of racism and white privilege in white communities has found a home not simply in the actual habits we have at Table, but in the shadows of avoidance and denial that afflict our segregated communities. These troubled memories take up a home place in us in a way that elides the normal practice of memory and its habit of being an integrated part of who we are. In this way, the memory and chronic experience of racism and white privilege follow the habits and patterns of trauma and, therefore, is an affliction that must be encountered with an eye toward the chaotic, unruly, and unconscious ways in which trauma wounds us in our flesh and blood. Traumatic memory haunts the Body of Christ with its repetitive playing out in segregated communities and through white obliviousness to racialized habituations.[38] These habits simultaneously embody return and

36. Lange, *Trauma Recalled*, 9.
37. Ibid., 15.
38. For a discussion of white obliviousness, see McClintock Fulkerson,

ignorance. How can we re-member the Body of Christ if we deny the wounds of the Body itself? Truly tending to the wounds of the Body, the memories that continue to diminish and distort the integrity of our narratives, will mean opening our memory and our deep connections up to transformative possibilities.

Re-membering is not simply a cognitive activity; it is an embodied dynamic. We come to Eucharist to remember our story and to re-member the Body of Christ in our communal act of sharing, proclaiming, ingesting bread and wine, and leaning on the mystery of God's transformative power to redeem and repair that which is most broken within us. Such communal memory and re-membering has the power to form and transform us. Liturgy has the capacity to embody both the practice of new habits and the impossibility of purely representational memory and narrative. Liturgy embodies the already and not yet of Christian identity and community. Trauma reveals and conceals the unavoidable disruption, aspirational integration, and strange conflation of past, present, and future.

How this harm inhabits us is unique and particular to each of us and to differently racialized groups; it is entangled in all of us. Our unique experiences, our shared social contexts, and our bodies' idiosyncrasies create in each of us particular and shared "tellings" of dis-membered stories of race.[39] The very character of bodies, racism, and church renders obvious variations in how different communities experience, acknowledge, and ignore these dynamics.[40] Trauma subtly habituates us in practices that tend to re-harm rather than re-form.

Places of Redemption.

39. See Mount Shoop, *Let the Bones Dance,* for an expanded discussion of the idiosyncratic ways the body "tells" embodied stories of harm, relationship, and ambiguity.

40. We are asserting that whiteness in this culture carries with it a particularly tenacious blindness to these dynamics. In turn, for instance, an all-black church may embody a different kind of awareness of the ravages of race that can be liberating. At the same time, both church demographics still "tell" in their own unique and particular ways of the dis-membered Body that our racist history has wrought. While the communities may be profoundly differently

Cathy Caruth explains that "the traumatic symptom cannot be interpreted, simply, as a distortion of reality, nor as the lending of unconscious meaning to a reality it wishes to ignore, nor as the repression of what once was wished."[41] Traumatic memory is a "literal return" of an event in a nonsymbolic mode. Trauma is a return of what actually happened in an arrested form. Caruth explains that "the traumatized . . . carry an impossible history within them, or they become themselves the symptom of a history that they cannot entirely possess."[42] The traumatic memory takes up a home place in each of us and in all of us in an involuntary and persistent mode that harms us all, even as it is uniquely held by those who occupy dissonant spaces in American culture. This memory replays and reifies the brokenness that gave it traction in our story in the first place. Traumatic memory replays its reality over and over again no matter how much the material reality it occupies has changed.

Racism and white privilege may seem to be things of the past because we can point to ways in which the material reality we occupy has changed. Civil rights, affirmative action, changing patterns of workplaces and neighborhoods, and a population that is becoming less white all point toward the different world we inhabit these days. Yet, the traumatic memory of the societal wounding is tenacious still in its ability to habituate practices and unconscious fears. Trauma possesses us, holds us captive as it is played out again and again in unconscious ways. We cannot heal from a dis-ease that lurks in places we ignore and deny. Caruth, referencing Freud, describes this ignorance and delay as a "latency" that is passed from generation to generation, condemned to repeat violence.[43]

Our eucharistic practice can show us our dis-ease. But traumatic memory can only give way to transformative practice when we surface dissonant truths about ourselves, as impossible as those

abled in their capacity for truth-telling around race, both are still deeply affected and even diminished by the dis-membered Body.

41. Caruth, "Introduction: Trauma and Experience," 5.

42. Ibid.

43. Caruth, *Unclaimed Experience*, 16–18.

15

truths may be. And life-giving truth makes space for communal flexibility, imagination, and connection. The full force of the violation "cries out," seeping through those who have little control over its emergence. Transformation, therefore, is not achieved by securing a correct or complete narrative but by making space for sporadic comprehension of the incomprehensible. Like the task of theology that seeks to assign language and description to the ineffable, healing liturgy around trauma defies full definition and demands embodied recognition.

The study of trauma invites us into the complicated wake of deep harm and how memory carries fragmented narratives, sensations, and woundedness into the present and future, into relationships and communities, and into the cells and habits of our bodies.[44] Traumatic memory loosens its chokehold on us when flexibility is introduced.[45] This flexibility can also create malleability around unconscious biases and oblivious privilege when it invites awareness of these dynamics to the surface. Flexibility learns to re-member by integrating traumatic memory into perspectives, frameworks, narratives, and embodied habits.[46] Flexibility also develops through the insertion of alternative imaginations into our narratives. Not being able to integrate the traumatic memory into the rest of one's life leads to a kind of dual existence and a "simultaneity" of traumatic experience that is "timeless" in its capacity to be palpably present.[47] Flexibility of memory introduces us to a space open to scenarios other than the trauma itself.

Flexibility, Imagination, and Connection as Transformative Eucharistic Practice

Flexibility, imagination, and connection do not elicit instant healing for the deep harms that trauma brings with it. Transforming

44. Van der Kolk and van der Hart, "Intrusive Past," 158–82.

45. Ibid., 178.

46. Van der Kolk and van der Hart describe this process as a repeated return to the memory in order to "complete it." Ibid., 176.

47. Ibid., 177.

memory is a complicated, promising, and mysterious possibility. These practices must be multilayered and include not just words but also embodied practices that wear new creek beds of thought, intuition, even unconscious instinct and reflex. Transforming collective memory around the communion table brings with it the added layers and complexity of multiple bodies and collections of unique constellations of being and understanding. Collective intentionality and shared practice become a necessity when we set ourselves to such profound change in our communities. Surely Jesus himself was doing similar work when he asked us to tell ourselves on a regular basis that we can be transformed into his dis-membered and re-membered Body through our gathering to chew on bread and share a cup.

In order for eucharistic practice to transform in the context of the traumatic memory of a racially dis-membered Body, churches will need to stretch into new postures and gestures of truth-telling and connection. How flexible are our gathered bodies when it comes to re-membering differently? The answer to that question can only be revealed in what "remains" we find in communities that truly imagine and practice a new kind of re-membering.[48]

Stretching into these new practices of flexibility, imagination, and connection will be idiosyncratic, located, and fluid. These practices will also help the church collectively continue to discern new habits of flexibility, imagination, and connection. The re-membered Body can enjoy vitality, even if its vitality is diminished by a past we find ways to acknowledge and integrate into who we are becoming. Particular healing intention around race will invite believing communities into some difficult and promising spaces together.

Our own cultural contexts as white Presbyterians and as women who have sought opportunities to help cultivate and experience cross-cultural community have kindled in us some impressions of healing possibilities. Transformation, in our reading of the biblical witness and Christian gospel, cannot be a monocultural

---

48. Shelly Rambo's *Spirit and Trauma* does beautiful, constructive work with the concept of what "remains."

dynamic even as we recognize the particular cultural growth edge that faces most white believers. Without intentional work by white faith communities to explore how we embody privilege and racialized biases in the habits of our faith, the transformative possibilities will be diminished and trivialized. Who we are will continue to be a story we tell ourselves, but a reality we seldom taste.

Many whites occupy a defensive posture when invited to excavate the way power and privilege function in their lives. Stories like "I didn't own slaves," or "my family may have been racist, but I'm not," create barriers to further exploration by suggesting that they are exempt from needing to examine these structures and habits.[49] Whites must face the continued realities of historic racism by means of a flexibility that allows them to stretch into a less defensive posture. Through learning and hearing other stories non-defensively, whites may have more room to name and claim their own. Room for the validity of dissonant stories can return our awareness to the ongoing violence we do not notice, and they can offer alternatives to whites being silenced by shame and guilt.

This flexibility is not simply about hearing and acknowledging diverse stories of others who have had experiences different than one's own. The transformative effect of flexible memory comes in seeing one's own past and present in a new way.[50] And the particular power of flexible memory to transform is deepened when we also recognize the impossibility of full comprehension. To address this relatively hidden form of brokenness, to re-member the past in a way that resonates with the complicated and distorted realities of racism's legacy, white churches need to acknowledge

49. See Bonilla-Silva, *Racism without Racists,* 53–102, for his account of the dominant stories whites tell. James Cone puts it more starkly: "People who have never been lynched by another group usually find it difficult to understand why blacks want whites to remember lynching atrocities. Why bring that up? Is it not best forgotten? Absolutely not! What happened to the hate that created the violence that lynched black people? Did it disappear?" *Cross and the Lynching Tree,* 164. His recent book is a moving account of the connection between brutal racism and the cross.

50. Shakti Butler's documentary *Mirrors of Privilege: Making Whiteness Visible* is a wonderful resource for hearing some of these stories of transformation among white people.

and explore white privilege. Many white churches express a kind of learned helplessness when it comes to working on issues of race. The common refrain is, "We've tried everything to be welcoming, and no people of color seem to come here." Many largely white churches have simply accepted their racial homogeneity as something they can't change because they can't attract people of color to be a substantive part of their communities.

New postures for white churches involve looking inward at the congregation itself instead of waiting for people of color to make real work on race possible. A new gesture might be to take an open stance toward exploring what it means to be white in American culture. These same gestures can be extended into congregations. Is there a way to name the harm that white communities embody because of their privilege? Is there a way to seek transformation within congregations that may cultivate a new kind of presence around race in our larger communities? These questions inform the aspirations of this project. We explore these possibilities by first surfacing the complexity of Eucharist, race, and memory in the chapters that follow.

Chapter 2 explores Eucharist as a template both for how our practices reenact the wounds of racism and privilege in white-dominant churches and for how our practices can provide healing opportunities for these same wounds. In chapter 3 we use the dynamics of colorblindness to surface the nature and depth of racism's wounds, particularly as these wounds become obscured and ignored in white-dominant communities. And in chapter 4 we unpack the complex dynamics of memory with particular attention to the mystery and tenacity of traumatic memory and how these dynamics express themselves in social, counter, and dangerous memory. Chapter 5 stitches together these three chapters into some suggestions, impressions, and vignettes about how flexibility and imagination around the communion table may help white-dominant churches to more profoundly embrace transformative practices when it comes to the wounds of race.

Re-membering a dis-membered Body is not formulaic or scientific. It is not about simple recollection or linear narrative.

Re-membering is a lived dynamic. And for any who have felt moments of this new sensation, for any who have glimpsed this vision of the Church "together in one place," you know the deep yearning for spaces and places for such re-membering to take hold. Those fleeting brushes with what can be change the stories we are able to tell and even the lives we are able to live. And the memories we make around the Table re-membered can be more vivid than any we have known thus far. Far from colorblind, we might finally have eyes to see and bodies that can be Christ's Technicolor dream for us.

two

Eucharist as Template: This Is My Body

TEMPLE: a place dedicated to the worship of a deity

PLATE: a flat sheet of metal, glass, or something similar, in which a picture has been etched or molded and used to print impressions on other surfaces

TEMPLATE: from *templet*; temple + plate; a pattern or mold that serves as a gauge

Eucharist tells us who we are even as it calls us to who God hopes we can be. Eucharist imprints us with meaning even as we help create impressions and reflections of our sacred identities, aspirations, and wounds. Engaging Eucharist as a potent disclosive template of our wounds *and* our possibilities invites first attention to patterns and impressions of the ritual that can serve to highlight its most compelling capacities. To surface what is compelling about Eucharist as both reflection of our distorted condition and impression of our redemptive capacity, we must attend to the limitations of our common liturgical practices around the Table and find windows into the potential for eucharistic practice to be healing. We are particularly interested in how Eucharist reflects, molds, and creates impression and possibility around the collective distortion of white colorblindness. Eucharist is a template through which we can see ourselves and the marks of racialized trauma more clearly. And Eucharist is also a mechanism that creates space for new reenactments that could integrate traumatic repetition and embodied practices with life-giving possibilities.

While biblical accounts do not provide an uncontested or pristine narrative of the origins of Eucharist, they do surface some fertile beginnings for our explorations of eucharistic possibilities and perils. Jesus' words and presence in some biblical accounts of the Eucharist provide us with a window into how the Body and bodies are invited and habituated in Eucharist. Biblical accounts of Jesus' Last Supper provide a prominent backdrop in eucharistic theology. In the synoptic accounts of the Last Supper, Jesus and his disciples are celebrating a Passover meal together.[1] In each of these accounts, there are clear descriptions of Jesus' concrete presence among his friends, the people he loved. And there are clear descriptions of betrayal and ruptured relationships. From its earliest expressions Eucharist held together this tension between a deep devotion and love for others and the pain of betrayal and broken community. Jesus invites his beloved to stay close to him even as he names the breach of trust that is unfolding before them.

In the Johanine account of this last meal, the supper is held before Passover and the focus is on Jesus' appropriation of a servant role among his disciples rather than on the bread and the cup.[2] Instead of bread and cup used to create connection and memory, the elements are referenced in the service of Jesus' recognition of the one who would betray him. According to John's Gospel, which lacks an account of the words of institution, on that last night of fellowship with his disciples Jesus washed their feet. And as he performed this act of service and care he told them who they needed to be in community by following his example. This incarnational account of the Last Supper is embodied in an act of servanthood and friendship. Foot-washing as understood in John's cultural context suggests that Jesus invited the sharing of Eucharist to be interpreted as a communal act of radical love.[3] And again in this account the embodied interdependence of beloved community

1. Matt 26:20–29; Mark 14:12–25; Luke 22:7–38.
2. John 13.
3. O'Day, "Sacraments of Friendship," 92–95.

also contains the stitches of remembered betrayal and ruptured relationship. The cultural backdrop of the Passover in all of these accounts also creates reverberations of memory around the sacred story of the exodus and God's liberative fidelity.

These sometimes dissonant marks of community that Jesus embodies and echoes in the biblical accounts of the Last Supper help mold our communal aspiration and rhetoric around the practice of Eucharist. Jesus is really present in this meal. And we remember Divine fidelity, love, justice, and liberation in the way we are together and in the intentions of our collective memory. And we also need to remember the tragic and violent marks of betrayal and ruptured relationship. The manner and model that Jesus provides in the earliest expressions of communion are also defined by the other examples of table fellowship we have from Jesus' life. Scholars assert that these other communal meals, including the many kinds of meals in which Jesus engaged during his ministry, contributed to the origin of the Eucharist. Throughout his life, Jesus typically ate with outsiders and identified with marginalized groups—from the poor and the unclean to women and the sick.

Other meals of Jesus' followers contribute to our inherited understanding of Eucharist, including the earliest post-resurrection meals.[4] And Paul's disappointment with the Corinthian church also provides us with glimpses of the practice and intention of Eucharist among Jesus' followers after his death.[5] Paul scolds the Corinthians for their distorted practice of Eucharist. They come together without dealing with the divisions that diminish the community. Those who get there first eat before the others have arrived. Some eat too much and even get drunk, while others get nothing. Paul fears that they approach the meal as a way to be satiated instead of as a proclamation of Jesus' death and resurrection. Paul exhorts the church in Corinth to be discerning around Christ's bodily presence in this meal and says, in effect, "If you are hungry, eat at home before you come."[6] The early church was called to

4. Berger, "Eucharistic Fragments," in *Gender Differences*, 67–93.

5. 1 Cor 11:17–34.

6. 1 Cor 11:34.

practice Eucharist as a revolutionary moment in time when Jesus was honored by equitable sharing and distribution of the elements and humble discernment about the presence of Christ's body in the community and its practices.

Biblical accounts provide us with a variety of markers for Eucharist, and celebrations of the Eucharist continued to morph and mold to different contexts and communities.[7] The early church celebration of Eucharist occurred in houses, an environment far different from the basilicas of later centuries. It is no surprise that the way the practices of ritual became increasingly complex and hierarchically structured in Constantinian times affected participants' sense of the function of Eucharist differently than the meal Jesus actually participated in.[8] These contexts and the way that they displayed and enacted Divine presence had a potent impact on how Eucharist was understood. The power of the eucharistic context to communicate and habituate the practices and performances of power continues to be important in how this ritual has its way with us and with our communities. And all of these early contexts bore the marks of Christ's real presence and the real presence of broken relationship and ruptured community.

The genealogy of church doctrine adds more layers to the ways in which we understand and practice Eucharist. In the context of the Roman Church the sacrament developed doctrinally with the help of Western philosophical influences into a ritual focused on the transubstantiation of bread and wine. The efficacy of the meal moved from the communal manner of sharing resources and performing equitable distribution of the elements toward a priestly moment in which the real presence of Christ was accomplished through the actual substance of the elements, the bread and the wine. The redemptive potency of Eucharist came to rest in the proper institutional performance of ritual in order for the substance of bread and wine to be transformed into the actual body

---

7. Foley, *From Age to Age*; Macy, *Treasures from the Storeroom*; Bradshaw, *Eucharistic Origins*; McGowan, *Ascetic Eucharists*.

8. For broad overviews of the meaning and function of Eucharist, see Morrill, *Anamnesis as Dangerous Memory*; Bieler and Schottroff, *Eucharist*.

and blood of Jesus Christ. Eucharist became not so much about participation in a communal embodied love as about inclusion in a ritual system that afforded the participants access to a singular redemptive reality.

This institutional expression of Eucharist became the object of protest and reform when the likes of Martin Luther and John Calvin staked their claim for a less priestly emphasis in Eucharist. Luther positioned himself as a resister of practices that reified the sacraments.[9] He offered a less substance-based interpretation of Christ's real presence in his description of consubstantiation. Christ is present in, around, and underneath the elements, but the elements themselves retain their substance. There is both Christ's real presence *and* real bread and wine after consecration of the elements. For John Calvin the argument from substance misplaced the transformative power of the meal in the priestly act. For Calvin, the power of the Holy Spirit, infused in the communal act of sharing Eucharist, is the means by which the transformation is achieved. Somehow in this mysterious power of Holy Spirit, the gathered community itself becomes the real Body of Christ. The church as gathered body is the location of real presence, not the elements themselves. For Calvin, this brought the emphasis back to the community, the way we share and distribute the elements, and the way we prepare ourselves and understand the intention of the meal. For Calvin the transformative potency of Eucharist was mysteriously, even mystically, accomplished by a community gathered in right relationship in Christ's name around this table of sacred memory.

A variety of interpretations and aspirations emerged from the common themes of the Reformation around Eucharist. Ulrich Zwingli's theology, for example, agreed with Luther's critique of the Aristotelian metaphysics of the bread and wine, but differed from Luther by understanding the celebration simply as a memorial. And even as remembering Jesus remained crucial, the nature of that remembering continued to find a variety of expressions. As the shifting contexts and rules for proper performance of

9. Lange, *Trauma Recalled*, 3–4.

Eucharist over the centuries reflect, material dynamics, power structures, affective postures, theological understandings, and bodily performance have a potent impact on how the sacrament is experienced. Formal ritual vestures worn in the context of Empire in spaces defined by power differentials will have different resonances and connotations than the meal on the street with people who are homeless.[10] The communion celebrations in Calvin's Geneva embodied their own particular kind of risk and resistance to institutional idolatry even as they helped construct the scaffolding of new power structures that likewise could exclude and diminish community. African American communion among enslaved people in the "hush harbors" of slave-owning communities had a distinct liberative capacity in its context.[11] These secret gatherings were rooted in what W. E. B. Du Bois would later call the enslaved community's "double consciousness." Remembering Jesus was embodied in the subversive community of liberation and care created in the hidden spaces where truths could be told among enslaved peoples. And remembering Jesus was embodied in the harsh realities of violence and abuse of power that defined the everyday lives of enslaved people.

Remembering Jesus in these different contexts carried with it the dissonance of the Divine promise of transformative community and the human reality of ruptured relationships and violence. And so the complexity of practicing and living into these aspirational themes and embodied realities and habituations is an essential part of our eucharistic heritage. Living into this heritage and promise requires careful attention to embodied place as well as liturgical formulae and theological traditions. The Body includes bodies that are complicated templates of power, oppression, healing, and brokenness themselves.

How does this complicated eucharistic framework overlay itself onto current practices of mainline Protestant communities today? We focus our gaze on the faith communities in which we have participated in Eucharist both as recipients and as officiants.

10. Saunders and Campbell, *Word on the Street*, 38–40.
11. Paris, "Theologies of Black Folk," 385–402.

As ordained Ministers of Word and Sacrament, or Teaching Elders, in the Presbyterian Church (U.S.A.), our experiences are drawn mostly from the variety of gathered communities we have inhabited in this denomination. While the Presbyterian ethos embodies its own particular kind of eucharistic dynamic, some of the patterns may provide sparks of recognition for those who practice in other denominational settings. The norms embodied in most Presbyterian eucharistic practices both remember a story of love and liberation and reenact our alienation from ourselves and from communities of difference.

The rhetoric and practices that define this sacramental meal in the Presbyterian tradition boast of communal transformation even as they reify our collective illusion that we are welcoming, inclusive, and transformative communities. Presbyterian eucharistic practice follows a common pattern that displays itself in an orderly, periodic, formalized community ritual during a service of worship. Eucharist is held most often on the first Sunday of the month. Many Presbyterian churches follow the liturgy in the *Book of Common Worship* and distribute the elements in a well-known style that any practiced Presbyterian can recognize. The officiating Elder at the Table, most often a Teaching Elder (Minister of Word and Sacrament), invites the congregation to the sacrament using the words given in the *Book of Common Worship*, usually closely reading them from a printed page. The Prayer of Great Thanksgiving follows the invitation, also often read from a printed version. In some congregations parts of the prayer will be interspersed with sung or spoken responses from the congregation. The Words of Institution follow, with the minister most often reading them, looking down at the page and then at the congregation or at the bread and cup, and then back down at the page. The congregants are told the following:

> The Lord Jesus, on the night of his arrest, took bread,
> and after giving thanks to God,
> he broke it, and gave it to his disciples, saying:
> Take, eat.
> This is my body, given for you.

Do this in remembrance of me.

In the same way he took the cup, saying:
This cup is the new covenant sealed in my blood,
shed for you for the forgiveness of sins.
Whenever you drink it,
do this in remembrance of me.

Every time you eat this bread and drink this cup,
you proclaim the saving death of the risen Lord,
until he comes.[12]

The communion of the people happens then commonly through a somber passing of the elements through the pews by designated Ruling Elders. The Elders pass the plates in a choreographed alternating pattern; congregants take their cube of bread and their thimbleful of grape juice and quietly follow instructions. Either we ingest the elements when they come to us or we carefully hold them one at a time to be taken when the officiating Elder indicates it is time for us all to partake together. In some communities people line up in the aisles to walk down to the front. There the officiants and assisting Elders stand together to serve the elements, one holding a loaf of bread, the other a cup filled with grape juice. As recipients come forward to receive communion, one by one they get a small piece of bread from one of the servers and then move to the next server, who lets them dip their bread in the cup of grape juice. In some settings the servers and members offer hand sanitizer to congregants as they approach the elements.

Often during communion quiet organ music plays or perhaps a hymn is sung. This music may help us feel less awkward or less self-conscious about our practice. Some people bow their heads in prayer, others look straight ahead, and still others appear to inspect the elements they've been given while they wait for the next step. We're told it's a joyful feast, but things are usually somber and we receive a tiny portion. We're told people come from everywhere to sit at this table, but we stay where we are and people who for the most part look a lot like us come and serve us with little emotion,

12. Presbyterian Church (U.S.A.), *Book of Common Worship*, 74–75.

with little connection. And we're told that Jesus said the bread was his body broken, the cup his blood poured out, but in such a sanitized environment that violence seems almost impossible to believe. From printed words on a page read while congregants follow along, to stiffened bodies quietly holding in their ambiguities and moderating their spiritual appetites, we're not sure what we're doing or what this sacrament could mean for us.

With muddled irregularity Presbyterians understand that we don't believe that the bread itself is Jesus' body or that the juice itself actually becomes blood. But even that theological distinction of Reformed theology does not create much space for a rich embodied embrace of the mystery and transformative potential of Eucharist. Instead, communities are left with a well-worn set of habits and little to show for it. If Eucharist is supposed to be a taste of God's kingdom, for many the kingdom may seem a lot like a staid hors d'oeuvres reception at the local country club. The pattern and form of typical eucharistic practice does little to coax us toward more inclusion, less rigidity, or seeing ourselves more clearly. The real presence of Jesus is not mentioned in the standard liturgy. Nor is the rupture that Jesus intentionally named in every scriptural tradition of the Last Supper that we have. And Calvin's theological mystery also seems far away from the predictable and formulaic practices of most Presbyterian congregations. Calvin's theology placed the real presence of Christ firmly and mysteriously in the flesh-and-blood bodies of the gathered community. This important transformative assertion about who the church is and can become, along with the mysterious and suggestive mode of getting us there, is not surfaced in the standard practice of Presbyterian Eucharist.

The violence of the originating event, a public execution of a religious leader, is far from the moderated movements of well-dressed professionals using sterling silver service. And the quiet ways that those gathered swallow the rhetoric of gathering at a table for all people while surrounded by, in most cases, almost total racial homogeneity can feed a systemic silencing around hard truths about privilege. Eucharist is a template for the dissonant narratives and practices of our faith communities. We occupy constrained spaces while telling ourselves that we are reaching out. We create sacrament out of sameness even while we profess God's call into a broader, more complicated world. And we embody a dangerous forgetfulness around the worst wounds of the world we live in even as we tell stories of liberation and reconciliation. We gather at the table of a Savior dismembered by violence even as we are invited to remember Him through a curiously sanitized gathering in a seemingly untroubled and safe space.

The Eucharist is not simply about reiterating a normative story; it is to have a performative effect for participants. The Eucharist is to perform or enact community in some way. This community is distinctively defined in relation to radical hospitality and beloved community lived out by Jesus and illustrated in his meals with outsiders and with his friends. And in such a distinctive community the iteration and performance of these narrated themes call out for more than just rote regurgitation of a well-known story; they call out for *liberative remembering*. Such remembering is crucial to the performance. It is remembering that somehow opens practitioners up to viewing the contemporary situation with a new capacity for liberative performance *in response to their particular situation*. The normative function of remembering in the ritual cannot be reduced to repetition. If it is to be faithful, it must somehow be dangerously truthful and subversive of the lies we tell ourselves. Eucharist invites memory and imagination for the transformative disruption of contemporary forms of brokenness.[13] And as "an expression of the experience of liberation given by God . . . remembering of the past is always about its relevance for current issues . . . [and requires] understanding the present."[14]

Physical place, bodily behavior, dress, habituation, and the basic cultural norms of Presbyterian practice are largely those of predominantly white, middle- to upper-middle-class communities. These habituations illustrate the bodily "proprieties" that are

13. The use of "dangerous memory" is attributed to Metz, *Faith in History. and Society,* 87–96. See also Scott, *Eucharist and Social Justice,* 70.

14. Bieler and Schottroff, *Eucharist,* 158f.

potent contributors to the reproduction of social identity.[15] An important kind of social, racial, and class identity appears to be reproduced in this ritual. The function of normative memory for the discernment and disruption of contemporary brokenness at the level of the social realities that come with privilege is, at best, obscured, and at worst nonfunctioning. While there is inevitably some sense of the contemporary situation in the experience of those who participate in this ritual in the fact that they are un-doubtedly aware of their own dilemmas and personal anxieties, and maybe even have awareness of their particular dilemmas around race as they take communion, this contemporary aware-ness begs a deeper question. What is the character and social significance of the contemporary situation that is being named and addressed in this contextual practice of Eucharist? How is the culture of these particular communities altered by the supposedly "dangerous memory" of the Jesus narrative? How does "remem-bering Jesus" in these contexts disrupt the contemporary situation of brokenness and function to disrupt rather than reproduce the dominant culture of white privilege? Without attention to these contextual realities and to the radical transformation that follow-ing Jesus invites in a racially divided culture, the Eucharist runs the risk of being merely the appreciative remembrance of a past act rather than a transformative practice that changes the way we live in the present.

If there is some way in which the Eucharist at its best might contribute to *re*-membering this communal reality in a trans-formative/redemptive way, then we must explore an alternative approach that surfaces the wound of colorblindness rather than simply referencing the normative past. To invite such communal awareness, we must give attention to a crucial missing piece: an analysis of the contemporary situation in relation to the wound of colorblindness. Transformative memory must surface the ways in which a social trauma such as racism is mediated through cultural representations and unconscious habitus. Transforming memory means that any collective memory that continues the practice of

15. Connerton, *How Societies Remember*, 82–88.

denial and avoidance of that harm must be disrupted and repurposed with new awareness, new habituations, and new horizons of imagination.[16]

The role of bodily habituations as shaped by cultural, class, race, and other social processes in the practice is crucial to this surfacing of new imaginations and habituations. To be the Body of Christ requires attention to real bodies—how they perform, communicate, and create new realities—not simply proper ritual, as in the following of the service of Word and Table via correct biblical passages, creeds, and doctrine. The bodily behaviors described in the common Presbyterian ritual of Eucharist are key to the performative effect of this remembering and to the contemporary situation that this "dangerous" remembering is supposedly discerning and addressing. How is the present practice and performance bound by the habits and patterns that embody denial of the trauma of ongoing racism? Can we collectively create the conditions for a new and creative theological imagination to emerge that might help alter the social wound of colorblindness?

16. An important resource for further discussion here is Eyerman, *Cultural Trauma*.

three

The Wound of Colorblindness

Let the peace of Christ rule in your hearts.
To this peace we were called
as members of a single body.
The peace of Christ be with you.[1]

F ar from being able to name and dress our collective wounds
around racism, many of the ways in which racism most af-
flicts the church remain concealed from our consciousness, and
sometimes even camouflaged as virtue. "When I look at a person,
I don't see color—I see a child of God" rolls off the tongues of
many Christians. These words are understood and embraced as
articulating the unbounded grace and generosity of God's love.
And through this aspiration of loving all people, regardless of their
demographic profile, many people have felt called to practice an
ethic of colorblindness.

This colorblind aspiration creates a necessary amnesia or
unknowing around racialized systems, histories, and bodies. And
this aspiration easily finds a home in communities deeply and often unconsciously shaped by whiteness and white culture. These
white-derived aspirations and habits are seamlessly coupled with
many of the common assumptions of privilege—that systems are
fair, that individuals are the center of how we understand rights

1. Words suggested in the *Book of Common Worship* for The Passing of the
Peace, which precedes Eucharist in worship. This language is drawn from Col.
3:15 and John 20:19, 21, 26.

and responsibilities, and that being educated in and conforming to societal norms is possible for everyone when they are given the "right tools." In the church these values manifest as mission statements and faith practices. And the resulting collective habituations and dispositions encouraged and practiced by churches focus on things like radical hospitality, service, and outreach to "the least of these."

Often, the rhetoric heard in mainline Protestant worship—from prayer, to sermon, to offering—reifies the assumption that everyone in church is called to help those in need. These people in need are described (sometimes subtly, other times not so subtly) as being outside the faith communities who seek to help them. "We" the church are helping "them" the poor, the disenfranchised, the oppressed, and the disadvantaged. These impulses toward service, charity, and outreach are taught as universal Christian virtues. The habituations and assumptions that they entail are not collectively explored in terms of race or social location. The stealthy affliction of colorblindness permeates faith communities with a fluid infiltration—it infects institutions of white culture, like the church, camouflaged as the very virtues to which we aspire as communities. And these virtues are not understood as culturally derived; they are to be exercised without regard to color and culture.

With reverberations of Paul Tillich's category of the demonic, the habits and practices of colorblindness distort and contort provisional goods by totalizing them, by being blind to their own finite and limited origins.[2] Tillich uses the fictional character of Faust to illustrate the demonic. Faust desires all knowledge and so makes a deal with the devil to know everything. Knowledge itself is not demonic; the desire to attain all knowledge, to collapse all of reality into oneself, is demonic. Colorblindness is blind to its own color, to its bias toward the absence of color. Colorblindness distorts a culturally derived value by making it an infinite value—a God-derived value. The language of colorblindness in the church takes the aspirations of whiteness to erase distinctions, to ignore

2. Tillich, *Systematic Theology*, 2:52

histories of oppression, and to bypass dissonant narratives and overlays them onto what God wants for us as people of faith.

God's kingdom, we hear again and again, is a place of unity. Christ's Body, we hear again and again, is a place where we are all one body. These aspirations of oneness and reconciliation are not necessarily demonic; blindness to the originary desire to make them in the image of white culture, however, obscures a demonic reality. These aspirations are instilled with a dangerous obliviousness to the power of whiteness and its habit of obscuring its own woundedness and its own capacity to wound. Surfacing the marks of colorblindness in eucharistic practice means inviting visibility where there has been invisibility. This invisibility has the capacity to conceal our collective wounds around race in plain sight. And our very stories, aspirations, and habituations geared toward overcoming racism are some of the dynamics that have increased its hold and its harm among us.

In this chapter we explore some of the ways in which this colorblindness is expressed and played out in white-dominant churches. These churches embody cultures that are largely white-derived and often regarded as normative or "normal." We will enlist the aid of various race theorists to help us surface some of the character traits of white culture. We will pay particular attention to how these character traits translate into practices and habituations in white-dominant churches. Both of us were formed in white-dominant church cultures, and we speak from and to those experiences and cultural systems. Defining such cultural habituations and practices is always complicated. To focus our attention in this complex descriptive work our discussions in this chapter and in the next are framed with two central normative eucharistic values: hospitality and remembering.

We interrogate both these normative eucharistic values through our learned color consciousness, particularly with our learned awareness of the problems with colorblindness. This learned color consciousness for both of us has been an intentional growth curve we have committed ourselves to through lived experience in relationships and communities that are cross-cultural, multiracial, and nonwhite dominant. That is, these relationships and communities have as central intentions both power-sharing and unmasking the concealed characteristics of white culture. We explore and interrogate the cultures that formed us with the perspectives we have gained from cultures and relationships that have shaped our race consciousness—particularly consciousness of some of the contours of white racialized identities. We realize our color consciousness will always be colored by the perspectives and experiences of whiteness, even with our best intentions at surfacing our unconscious biases and blind spots. We also realize that good intentions do not necessarily get to the layers of woundedness that are in most need of healing. In those crevices of continued obliviousness, we continue to pray for the Spirit's generosity to invite us in a healing direction.

Both our experiences and our continued need for growth and transformation are full-bodied phenomena. These dynamics are shaped by the multiple layers of embodied existence. And bodies are formed and transformed through habituations and dispositions that arise from these same layers of who we are, what we inherit, and who we aspire to be. The character of these habituations and dispositions will emerge as we describe the following five particular habits prevalent in white-dominant churches.

Five Habits of White-Dominant Churches: On Constructing Colorblind Communities

Five habits associated with colorblind community formation surface when we seek to name and address the wounds of race in churches today. These habits and practices can appear to reflect positive values and beliefs about community formation. And they can, in fact, serve to further entrench the dominance of white culture. Since colorblindness, especially in the context of church, is understood in white-dominant churches to be an ethically preferred attitude toward persons of color, these practices and convictions are frequently understood as universal Christian virtues and regarded as liberating and faithful aspirations. The five habits we explore here are all embodied and practiced in many layers of church life. They are, however, also a profound in-forming force in the way eucharistic practices, in particular, are embodied and practiced.

Habit One: The Lord's Supper Takes After Jesus

The first habit springs from understanding the Eucharist, or the Lord's Supper, as modeled after Jesus' practices and ministry. Jesus ate with sinners and welcomed all to his table, including outsiders, the clean and the unclean. Jesus crossed social boundaries. He had friendships and conversations with women that were taboo (the Syro-Phoenician woman, the woman at the well, the woman who anointed his head with oil, Mary Magdalene, etc.). The Lord's Supper is the celebration and reenactment of Jesus' radical hospitality—the Jesus who ate with outsiders and identified with the oppressed.[3]

The radical vision enacted by Jesus' ministry has for centuries been claimed and invoked by many, even as its enactment is much more difficult to put into practice. Professional journalist Sara Miles calls the Eucharist a "contradictory package of Christianity."[4] Miles converted to Christianity precisely *because* of the vision of radical hospitality she discerned in the communion ritual. Her years of work with homeless people led her to invite her new church community to regard food pantry distribution and meals with the homeless as eucharistic practices. She described this work as centering around "a hunger that had to do with the bodies of strangers, with offering everything we had, giving away control, and receiving what we needed to live. Communion." In response to her request to make the food pantry part of Sunday Eucharist, she got strong negative responses. The church saw feeding the hungry as one thing, but "real church" was something very dif-

3. Some of the liberation-oriented theologians who connect Eucharist with social justice are Frederick Herzog, Gustavo Gutiérrez, Leonardo Boff, Jon Sobrino, and M. Shawn Copeland.

4. Miles, *Take This Bread*, 76.

ferent.[5] Miles' conclusion: as "[a] sign of unconditional acceptance and forgiveness," the Eucharist "was doled out and rationed to insiders."[6]

The "real church" Miles encountered does not reflect the practices of all faith communities, but statistics bear out a common pattern among white-dominant churches—that of tending to form communities of people who "look like us" rather than engaging in the radical hospitality that Jesus modeled in his ministry. People at the Protestant table are overwhelmingly of the same race. Results of a 2009 study by the Pew Forum on Religion & Public Life on "the racial composition" of Christian churches indicates that they "remain predominantly white and lag behind the general population in terms of racial diversity." Defining "white" in contrast to persons of color and Hispanics, the study found that mainline Protestant churches have the highest percentage of racial homogeneity, with 91 percent being white; next come Orthodox churches at 87 percent, then Evangelical Protestant churches, which are 81 percent white. Roman Catholics are the most racially diverse, being 65 percent white and 29 percent Hispanic.[7]

So we mainline Protestants mostly gather together at the table with bodies that pretty much look like our own. We may *invoke* all others in the manner of the ritual invitation—"They will come from east and west, and from north and south"[8]—but those gathered at the table actually embody an accepted homogeneity. This radical welcome is a eucharistic mantra of white-dominant communities even as the real bodies of "others" are most frequently there as aspirations/apparitions—ghosts of communities Jesus occupied and of painful societal ruptures that we want to believe have been healed. Jesus' radical hospitality at the table, no matter how much white-dominant churches invoke it, is not a common

5. Ibid., 249, 251.

6. "A sign of unity, it divided people; a sign of the most common and ordinary human reality, it was rarefied and theorized nearly to death." Ibid, 76.

7. Cited in Robinson, *Race and Theology*, 81.

8. Presbyterian Church (U.S.A.), *Book of Common Worship*, 68.

embodied practice at actual tables of communion in most American churches.

Habit Two: "Normal People Don't Have a Culture" or Norming White Ways as the Best Ways

A second habit of white-dominant churches is universalizing or norming that church's culture. Maggie Potapchuk lists this norming habit as the number one trait of white culture: "White culture defines what is considered normal—it creates the standard for judging values."[9] This habit is expressed in familiar turns of phrase: "This is regular church," or "We're just ordinary people," or "Everyone is welcome here."

White norming habits tend to understand white-dominant institutions as "regular." That white-dominant churches understand themselves to be "regular church" is not surprising. People in the dominant culture do not typically think of their community as the outlier, the heretical community, or the dissenter group. And being regular or "normal" faithful people does not mean an absence of standards; it means normalizing your standards. What is normal faith is the "real thing" as opposed to something requiring recognition of a specific culture or as an "alternative" vision or experience. While denominational loyalties are acknowledged, beliefs, commitments, practices, and habits of most white-dominant churches do not require attention to or acknowledgment of their cultural derivation.

This cultural obliviousness is only interrupted in white-dominant churches when someone is present who represents a "marked" group. Then there may be space granted for acknowledgment of those who are seen as having culture. For example, the Presbyterian Church (U.S.A.) denominational structure recognizes multicultural churches at the national level with their Office of Multicultural Congregational Support (OMCS).[10] The PC

9. Potapchuk, "White Culture Handout."

10. During the editing of this book the PC (U.S.A.) eliminated the OMCS. It is unclear if or how the programs and initiatives of that office will be carried

(U.S.A.) also has the Presbyterian Intercultural Network (PIN) that connects multicultural churches with churches that wish to be more multicultural through a grassroots network. The OMCS was located organizationally in the Office of Racial Ethnic and Women's Ministries. These cross-cultural and multiracial churches take their place alongside the offices that advocate for and support the concerns of several different constituencies that the denomination labels as "racial/ethnic." Black/African American, Native American, Korean, and Latino/a constituencies have staff members and offices to support them as well as grassroots caucuses.

This organizational structure displays the habit of racializing the ethnic origins of people of color over and against the normed "regular" churches that are white-dominant. Groups with "ethnicity," such as Hispanics and Koreans, are thus recognized as having cultures, while whites are "unraced." There is no "white caucus." As the dominant race, there would seem to be no need for a caucus. However, the failure to identify whiteness as a "race" with a culture is an element of the unacknowledged power and privilege of whiteness.

While culture can be defined in a variety of ways—from civilization to a distinctive, elite "high art"—we are using a common definition that signals preferred values, symbols, aesthetics, and practices that are experienced as what is "proper."[11] Our earlier description of the common communion practice in white-dominant Presbyterian churches is illustrative. For instance, white-dominant Presbyterian culture encourages a particular tone and protocol for eucharistic practice. Presbyterian communion liturgy and practice tends to be somber and controlled. There are shared cultural expectations around appropriate clothing and certain kinds of music. Often tiny cubes of bread and small cups of grape juice (instituted

---

forward. The Presbyterian Mission Agency has an employee designated for "cross-cultural" ministries and now has an office designated for intercultural ministries. While time will tell how this new nomenclature and staffing hits the ground in congregations, there remain profound questions about how whiteness is attended to by the church. "Race" continues to be a designation largely used for nonwhites in the program structure of the denomination.

11. Williams, *Keywords*, 87–93.

by Presbyterians in the early nineteenth century in the northeast for fear of germs from the common cup) are the preferred material forms of the sacramental elements. While there may be some variation in practice around the Presbyterian church, such as using a common loaf, a common cup, and intinction as the mode of sharing the elements, the somber and orderly practice of Eucharist is something familiar and "normal" for any seasoned Presbyterian. As "normal" as this seems to Presbyterians, any ritual, however normative and requisite, is always already shaped by a particular culture, even when unacknowledged. Overlapping symbols are expressed materially, aesthetically, and practically by communities due to their assumptions regarding what is normal. These practices, habits, assumptions, and expectations are *culture*.[12]

Failing to acknowledge one's culture can conceal its power to dominate and to erase. And in white-dominant churches this lack of acknowledgment comes with the claim that we welcome all people. Being blind to culture, however, deeply affects the kind of welcoming that happens. Even multicultural churches that embody diversity tend to require assimilation into white-derived cultural worship practices.[13] Assimilation is a prominent tactic for dominant groups as they enhance their "diversity." And the desire for conformity to community practices assumes that the dominant culture is the desired, normative way to live and worship. While such norming is a common characteristic of most cultural expressions, the obliviousness to the fact that the norms emerge from a culture is most often expressed in communities of the dominant race.

While being a "regular church" that welcomes all people sounds faithful, it can conceal a wounding reality.

---

12. Of course, culture is impacted by other crucial factors, such as institutional structures and economic systems. Raymond Williams' work on culture was developed in relation to the role of capitalism in the shaping of lives. See Williams, *Keywords*; Williams, *Culture and Materialism*; Williams, *Culture and Society, 1780–1950*.

13. Edwards, *Elusive Dream*, 117–40.

Habit Three: "We Are All God's Children" (and Our Differences Don't Matter)

"We are all God's children": this sentiment is held up as both a treasured value of Christian community and a God-instilled aspiration. The great equalizer of our common Creator is supposed to help us embrace and live into our sameness, our unity, and our connection to one another through the Divine stitching that makes us who we really are. And because of this common origin, we can let go of our fear and judgment based on differences that tend to divide human communities—race, class, sexual orientation, and beliefs, to name a few. And this great equalizer of our created nature is supposed to make those differences insignificant and secondary to what truly creates community and connection. In the midst of conflict, in the midst of turmoil, churches often invoke this mark of the church's identity: it is our sameness that creates the ties that bind, not our difference.

This treasured value of sameness, this God-instilled aspiration of making differences insignificant to the connective tissue of a community, invites the cultivation of certain habits and dispositions. And in white-dominant churches these habits and dispositions create what are often unconscious instincts about how those who present as "different" from the norm are welcomed into the community's life. Welcoming expresses itself in a choreographed system of one-size-fits-all hospitality. Everyone gets a smile and a hello from the greeter at the door. Everyone gets a word of welcome from the pastor and in the bulletin. Everyone is invited to sign the pew pads. Everyone who shares her address receives a letter of welcome inviting her to come back or even to consider membership. As mainline churches shrink in size, these habits of systematic hospitality have been scrutinized, updated, shored up, and adjusted to try to get new members in the door.

Underneath these expressions of hospitality that churches proudly extend to "all God's children" lie the expectations of conformity that accompany them. These expectations are rooted in white culture's norming of values, manners, etiquette, worship styles, modes of spiritual experience, dress . . . the list goes on and on. All God's children are kindly welcome. And surely all God's children know how to act in church! At one multicultural church a deacon shared her discomfort with the pastor when several members of a Holiness church attended the church's Presbyterian worship service. She shared that she "didn't have a problem" with them coming to church "if they know how to act." When pressed by her pastor to say exactly what that meant to her, she said that their clapping and speaking out during worship, and the fact that they brought a tambourine, were "disrespectful" and "disruptive." Her understanding was that "all are welcome" and they need to "act appropriately" in church. This disposition toward differences as incidental and not the core of our welcoming impulse masked expectations around conformity and white dominance.

The complicated truth is that differences matter in church. And the often unexamined expectation is that differences are to disappear when we cross the threshold of a sanctuary. This aspiration of unity and sameness has also authorized the expectation of conformity to the unnamed cultural expectations of white culture. Churchgoers are often expected to no longer embody culture or idiosyncrasy; we are to shed those aspects of our identity and conform to the "right" and "appropriate" behaviors for being in church. These manners and mannerisms are available, the church assumes, to everyone and therefore not a barrier to feeling welcome. White culture habituates obliviousness around how talk of sameness can be diminishing and unwelcoming to those who do not or cannot conform to the unspoken expectations of church-appropriate behavior. The constrained spaces these expectations create help cultivate an environment that is quietly hostile to cultural diversity and spiritual idiosyncrasy.

Habit Four: We Are the Body of Christ

A fourth habit of white-dominant churches is rooted in a disconnect between our theological understanding of bodies and the realities of our embodied existence. Even as we call ourselves the

"Body of Christ," white-dominant churches especially struggle to live into an incarnational mode of being church.[14] Bodies are marginalized in typical worship forms as well as in the liturgical language most commonly used in white-dominant churches. In mainline Protestant expressions of church, the worship and liturgical experience tends to be more cerebral than embodied, with the focus on the spoken word and the teaching of the sermon. Bodies are asked to do very little except be still, stand up, and sit down at designated times. In many white-dominated churches there is a hypervigilance around avoiding the complexity, ambiguity, and mystery of bodies. This avoidance manifests itself in habits ranging from strategically placing hand sanitizer so that all use it prior to entering the sanctuary or taking communion, to the tightly choreographed flow of worship ("decently and in order," in the Presbyterian tradition) scripted in the order of worship, to the polite invitation to leave the sanctuary with crying children printed prominently in the bulletin. This avoidance of real bodies, as we have already described, seeps into common communion practices as well.

Even with the prominence of "Body of Christ" language and ideas, the dispositions of actual bodies in white-dominant churches do more to discourage connection and intimacy with God's mystery than they do to encourage those experiences. Rather than open up space for brushes with the Divine, the mystery of spiritual community is filtered through systems and habits that discourage novelty and surprise. Bodily habits that contradict the honoring of actual bodies are expressed in those habits already mentioned, such as the disconnect between white-dominant churches' claims of radical welcome and their typical practice of "community" with bodies like their own. But concern about how bodies matter is not just acknowledging which bodies are there or not there; making space for bodies to truly matter requires attending to the crucial role of bodily *habituations* and dispositions that underlie such racial and other "segregations."

14. Mount Shoop, *Let the Bones Dance.*

Bodily habituations are the typically unacknowledged, pre-reflective habits or routinized "knowledges" that make up our everyday lives. Habituations are ways of being-in-the-world, including bodily skills that we need to get through life. They also include enculturated habits of attraction and comfort, along with aversions to and discomfort with different realities. These habits are typically shaped by our social groups. As Pierre Bourdieu puts it, we are "socially informed bodies" most at home with bodies of our social location.[15]

A disposition is "an inclination that includes outlook, attitude, and tendencies toward certain behaviors" that will "integrate all layers of embodied experience."[16] Dispositions embody and perform the idiosyncratic ways in which bodies habituate and perform all that makes up their experience. Each body uniquely embodies and expresses its own inheritance even as each body has the capacity to practice, learn, and reshape how it "disposes" of itself. Dispositions "integrate all layers of embodied experience. They are not only ethical, but also existential and deeply embedded beyond the reach of conscious decision. Bodies feel and fashion inclinations, behaviors, outlooks, and character out of the constellations of feeling's flow."[17]

As pre-reflective, unconscious "knowledges," habituations and dispositions include prejudices, reactions, and impulses that commonly are unexamined. For example, white habitus is "a set of primary networks and associations with other whites" that entail dispositions of comfort with certain kinds of bodies, typically white bodies "like us," and discomfort with bodies that are different. The persistent prominence of what is called the "white

---

15. Habitus takes the form of "a system of lasting, transposable dispositions which, integrating past experiences, function at every moment as a *matrix of perceptions, appreciations, and actions* and make possible the achievement of infinitely diversified tasks," durable dispositions that re-externalize social cultures in ever-new ways. Bourdieu, *Outline of a Theory of Practice*, 16f. For discussion of the adequacy of his account of change, see Calhoun, "Habitus, Field, and Capital," 61–88.

16. Mount Shoop, *Let the Bones Dance*, 129

17. Ibid.

bubble"—the lack of significant, face-to-face, ongoing contact by whites with persons of color—is a crucial factor in shaping white habituations and dispositions.[18]

Many studies show that whites still prefer to live in all-white or predominantly white neighborhoods.[19] Stories abound that illustrate white habits of bodily habituation relative to racialized perceptions. When there is a dearth of significant kinds of contact that could challenge racial stereotypes, they continue to have a profound impact.[20] Stereotypes of black male bodies often shape white responses of fear when whites encounter black males while walking downtown at night, for example, or the common stereotype at work in racial profiling by law enforcement of "driving while black." While these fears and suspicions can obviously become beliefs, the importance of attention to habituation is that the reactions initially occur due to deeply embedded unconscious dispositions toward certain kinds of bodies.

Multiracial churches also have white members who can and do react to bodies of color in ways that contradict their convictions

18. During the writing of this book the Michael Brown shooting occurred in Ferguson, Missouri, and a wave of protests around the country (and even the world) followed the grand jury's failure to indict Darren Wilson, the police officer who shot Brown. During this time the Public Religion Research Institute (PRRI) did an important study on white perceptions of fairness, the results of which can be found online: http://publicreligion.org/research/graphic-of-the-week/americans-racial-disconnect-on-fairness-and-discrimination/. The PRRI also did a study on white-dominated social networks; for the results of that study, see http://publicreligion.org/research/2014/08/analysis-social-network/.

19. According to Melanie E. L. Bush, one study "shows that whites avoid living in neighborhoods with more than a small Black population because they associate Blacks with high crime, low housing values, and low-quality education." *Breaking the Code*, 4f.

20. Feagin and O'Brien say we need to attend to what Toni Morrison called the "white problem" rather than continuing to consider race to be a problem for people of color: "Most whites still do not see the problem of 'race' in America as a 'white problem.'" Crucial to this is "the fact that most whites live in what might be termed the 'white bubble'—that is, they live out lives generally isolated from sustained and intensive equal-status contacts with African Americans and other Americans of color." Feagin and O'Brien, *White Men on Race*, 5, 25.

about inclusiveness. Some members resist having a minister of color, illustrating a disconnect between the belief in the good of racial diversity and the actual bodily habituations of the dominant group.[21] One account of an intentionally interracial church with a white minister tells of how some white members complained that the church was becoming "too black" when a black African friend of the white minister preached in his place and a number of his black friends came to worship. While there were never more persons of color than whites in regular attendance, some of the whites left as a result. This departure is very likely rooted in some white aversive bodily reactions to what was *perceived* as "black dominance," since their complaint was not based upon facts.[22]

The increasing attention given by scholars to the role of bodies in our liturgical practice as the Body of Christ inadvertently enhances the importance of these supposedly unintentional white-dominant habits.[23] Liturgical scholars now often emphasize that liturgy and worship are not simply cognitive but both formative of and deeply linked to "our desires, emotions, attitudes, beliefs and actions," and it is crucial, says Don Saliers, to emphasize affections as well as virtues formed.[24] Furthermore, bodies matter and cannot be reduced to the claimed belief or emotions that come with their actions and movements. "Bodily gestures do not merely 'describe an attitude,' they enact the relationship described by that attitude."[25] John F. Baldovin SJ says, "One of the (many) functions that rituals (and therefore liturgy) perform is to help a group of people experience solidarity, identity and common purpose. And

---

21. Edwards, *Elusive Dream,* 56–82.

22. McClintock Fulkerson, *Places of Redemption,* 80–88.

23. Baldovin does not bring up race, class, gender, and other forms of cultural habituation, but some liturgical scholars are explicit in connecting markers such as race, gender, and class to the bodies performing Eucharist. See Bieler, *Eucharist;* Morrill, *Anamnesis as Dangerous Memory;* Keshgegian, *Redeeming Memories;* Copeland, *Enfleshing Freedom,* 231–52.

24. Saliers, "Liturgy and Ethics," 16f.

25. Leonard, *Postures of the Assembly,* v.

the very reason they need ritual is to express that identity *bodily* and *communally*."[26]

Baldovin's comments highlighting the crucial function of bodily performance simply confirm the harm being done. Whatever else it may do, white-dominant worship will certainly reproduce our deeply embedded bodily connections with white people. For white-dominant churches, "who we are as a community in the presence of the living God" is the Body of Christ with racial privilege and power, and our ritual performance helps us "experience solidarity, identity and common purpose" as that white Body.[27]

Habit Five: *Imago Dei* and Sinfulness

A final habit in white-dominant churches has to do with common narratives of sin and redemption. These narratives are primarily understood as the work of the Trinitarian God (most often named as Father, Son, and Holy Spirit). The interesting layer here for our exploration of white habits is the theological anthropology (the understanding of the human being) that emerges from these narratives. The *Book of Common Worship* has communion liturgy that reiterates this Trinitarian understanding of God and brings with it

26. Baldovin, "Embodied Eucharistic Prayer," 3.

27. Baldovin continues, "My point here is not to persuade people to sign themselves with the cross at the liturgical proclamation of the gospel so much as it is to argue that what we do communally with our bodies at worship makes a great deal of difference when it comes to one of the main reasons for public worship in the first place—namely, to express who we are as a community in the presence of the living God." And, "it is not for no reason that the Orthodox have been characterized as 'the church standing,' the Roman Catholics as 'the church kneeling' and the Protestants as 'the church sitting.' These basic bodily postures communicate a great deal about the self-identity of these Christian communions. Though none of these postures is exclusive to the church that it characterizes, each one tells us something about basic attitudes: standing as praising God with upright bodies, kneeling as an act either of adoration or of penitence, and sitting as an act of receptivity, listening and participating in a common meal. Each posture certainly has its advantages, and each makes a great deal of difference in the self-understanding of the church." "Embodied Eucharistic Prayer," 3.

a view of human beings best understood if we view this narrative relative to God's actions. The creating, redeeming, and sustaining work of God entails a view of human beings as created in the image of God, broken by sin, and redeemed by the life, death, and resurrection of Jesus Christ. This redemption is cultivated, sanctified, and embodied through faithful living. And this narrative comes complete with the eschatological hope for the future realization of the kingdom of God, in which all of creation can live into who we were made to be.

Specific versions of this traditional view of human beings as created in the image of God, as sinful, and as being redeemed vary, however. And in some expressions of the narrative we can surface some dynamics that contribute to the cultivation of dangerous and harmful habits in white-dominant communities. A focus on sin is illustrative. Practiced liturgically in the form of confession, for actual communities sin can be further specified as breaking particular rules, being immoral or "unfaithful," or not being "biblical," among other things. Assumptions about the *imago Dei* and where exactly it is "located" in our sinful condition matter. For instance, some communities think dualistically, locating our *imago Dei* in the soul, not the body. The body is understood as the problem, the seat of desire, the reason for sin, and not as an expression of the ways we were created in God's image. Not far underneath this distancing of God's image in our created nature from our embodied existence is a profound ambivalence about the worth and dignity of any body. If one cannot embrace and love one's own body as created good, as sacred, then it is hard to love the bodies of others, especially others whom cultural messages have taught us to fear or to see as inferior.

In many Protestant theological traditions, self-denial and the diminishment of the self are not seen as problems to solve but instead are considered virtues, especially for women. Doctrines of sin as pride or self-absorption reinforce the mentality that the embodied self is a problem and needs to be diminished. These narratives of sin create conditions ripe for self-loathing and guilt. And this guilt and self-loathing can even be regarded as sign and seal of knowing one's place in the order of things, as virtues of Christian piety. While it may be hard to see that self-loathing is a concern worth exploring in communities dominated by those who enjoy the privileges of race, this deep ambivalence about the self may be the root cause of some of the most harmful habits of whiteness. This sanctified self-loathing can also camouflage some of the spiritual deficits of white-dominant communities that keep them in an arrested space, unable to examine themselves with enough nuance to truly explore and accept truths about whiteness.[28]

This acceptance does not mean whitewashing the legacy of slavery, racism, and privilege, but it could clear space for a more honest and complicated understanding of whiteness, including the dynamics of white privilege and sin. James Baldwin saw the deep connection between honoring our own *imago Dei* and our capacity to honor that same image in the other: "White people in this country will have quite enough to do in learning how to accept and love themselves and each other, and when they have achieved this—which will not be tomorrow and may very well be never—the Negro problem will no longer exist, for it will no longer be needed."[29]

This lack of self-love and the resulting lack of self-understanding and self-consciousness in white-dominant faith communities have trivialized the narratives of sin most often operative. While Reformed theological traditions distinguished themselves from a perceived individualistic approach to sin and forgiveness in the Roman Church's confessional system, replacing that system with a corporate confession has further concealed some problems when it comes to naming systemic sin. The corporate confession common in much Reformed worship suggests that we all share the same sinful human profile—our failings include leaving things undone that needed to be done, neglecting to be generous, and tending to focus on ourselves—but shared shortcomings cannot be equated with systemic manifestations of sin. For instance, racism, according to

28. Sullivan discusses the importance of white self-love in *Good White People*, 9.

29. Quoted in ibid., 9f.

this narrative of sin in Reformed theology, might be described as a hateful act by an individual toward a person based on race, as the failure of a community to be welcoming, or as a fear of people who are different than we are. These expressions of sin inherent in racism may be things lots of people do, but these descriptions do not surface the systems in place that create racialized disadvantage and advantage. Nor do they surface the way in which power is used to create such systems of advantage and disadvantage. There may be a collective confession, but there is little or no attention given to systems and to how white supremacy and dominance gave rise to many of those systems.

These narratives of sin, as well as the narratives of our created nature, which are common in white-dominant churches, create a culture of avoidance when it comes to what we really fear. Fear of the ambiguity of life is, indeed, the "root of idolatry."[30] Systems of achievement can help create the illusion that ambiguity can be avoided or neutralized and that there is no such thing as systemically created disadvantage. One's failure is due to aspects of one's character, not to distortions of the systems that create advantage. And when it comes to culpability and achievement, these systems we believe to be accessible and fair allow us to focus our gaze on individuals rather than on the whence of the systems.

The naming of brokenness in terms of structures, power dimensions, and harms, however, is rarely fleshed out in liturgy. With the exception of prayers for harmed groups or topics discussed in the occasional sermon, references to outsiders like the poor, the oppressed, and the marginalized do not include a contextual interpretation of the contemporary space and social location of a church. The trivialized and contorted understanding of the human being as made in God's image (but we are not sure how) and diseased by sin (and therefore unworthy of redemption, though given it anyway purely by God's grace) does not leave much space for these systems to tell us about who we are and how our cultural habits and assumptions might be sources of harm or diminishment in human society. The image of God in us is trotted

---

30. Mount Shoop, *Let the Bones Dance*, 118.

out periodically as a way to bless the places where we collectively recognize beloved community taking shape and Christian virtues being practiced. Our understanding of those community traits and personal characteristics varies, but generally refers to things such as self-sacrifice, humility, putting one's needs behind the needs of others, generosity, kindness, helping the least of these, obeying the rules, and doing things "decently and in order." And so the healing needs of the world are "out there" in the lives of those "less fortunate." And white-dominant churches understand themselves as those who help those in need, not those in need of help.

This habit gives rise to all sorts of collective habits of engagement and avoidance. White-dominant churches, for instance, can generate lots of energy and enthusiasm around helping people of color in other places, like Africa and Haiti, rather than being involved directly in the challenges many people of color face in the United States, even in the neighborhoods where the churches themselves are located. A prominent white Presbyterian church in North Carolina that claims to be inclusive has its biggest investment in ministries in Africa. While outreach to Africa is not a bad thing—poverty in Africa is severe, and addressing this and other issues is crucially important—the well-worn path to such modes of engagement for the church raises several questions around how we understand ourselves as the church in a larger context and community. How and when is this engagement a way of avoiding some of the more uncomfortable elements of racialization when persons of color in our own towns, even in the poorest neighborhoods not too far from our white-dominant churches, are not on the church's radar?

Beyond the question of how the church decides where to focus its mission is the question of how the church situates itself in the contexts in which it finds itself. And what space is there for the work white-dominant churches need to do in order to cultivate the kind of self-awareness necessary to engage in substantive relationships across boundaries of race and privilege in their own contexts? If the church is only reaching out to help, with no understanding of needing help itself, these relationships will most often serve to reify concentrations of power and privilege. And even while this habit of "helping the others" can reinforce a sense of privilege and power, it is never that simple.

The narratives of *imago Dei* and sin do little to invite a more complicated way of understanding ourselves. Instead, whiteness habituates a protected space in which these complexities and ambiguities can be avoided and the church's work can focus on "the less fortunate."

Acknowledging Wounds

These five habits of white-dominant churches help to surface wounds that have been largely concealed, both because of avoidance and because of the way in which white culture seamlessly extrapolates universal virtue from culturally derived norms and biases. "When I look at a person, I don't see color—I see a child of God" echoes the ethos of colorblindness as Christian virtue. The unacknowledged wounds of racism and racialized mentalities fester beneath the surface of feigned well-being. And the concealment of wounds expresses itself in the mission of the church to "reach out" with generosity to those who have real needs. White-dominant churches are not the ones in need of healing—the rest of the world is.

This colorblind aspiration embodies obliviousness to racialized systems, histories, and bodies, and to the danger of obliviousness itself. Moreover, this aspiration is a common companion to understandings of Christian mission and ethics in communities deeply and often unconsciously shaped by whiteness and white culture. These values shape mission, practices, habits, and dispositions. And—even more difficult to see—this aspiration shapes self-understandings and unconscious assumptions of white-dominant churches. The five habits we explored above helped surface the wounds of colorblindness in the way hospitality is practiced in Eucharist. The next chapter invites the same surfacing around the dynamics of eucharistic remembering.

four

Transforming Memory

This is my body, which is given for you. Do this in
remembrance of me.

—LUKE 22:19

Jesus' words to his friends and followers at the Last Supper continue to beckon to the table those who love him in this mode
of remembering. This disposition of memory, however, is not a
simple set of words or a settled story to recall. Eucharistic memory
is dynamic, embodied, and invitational. The practice of Eucharist
invites its practitioners to connect to Jesus' words and stories in
ways that change who we are and how we live in the world today.
And this practice is complicated and contextual, as it reflects who
we are and how we live.

Indeed, eucharistic memory is not simply about recalling
Jesus' story or reading the correct biblical passages and official
denominational liturgy to recover pieces of the past. Recall alone
is "nostalgic or fetishistic memory."[1] This eucharistic memory is
much more than simple recall; it is to be transformative and dynamic.[2] In contrast to nostalgic memory, the biblical tradition
presents memory of the past to be "always about its relevance for

1. Bieler and Schottroff, *Eucharist,* 166.

2. Keshgegian puts it quite clearly: "Remembering is not meant to enshrine
a memorial but to point to and effect present action." *Redeeming Memories,* 25.

current issues . . . [and for] understanding the present."[3] Likewise, eucharistic memory is about remembering Jesus' life, ministry, death, and resurrection for the sake of understanding how God is calling us to address the present context and its brokenness.[4]

The nature of eucharistic remembering was pivotal in the unfolding of the Reformation. Calvin placed profound importance on the nature of collective remembering and its transformative power for the community. Eucharist was not just about recalling a story but also about the community's being transformed into the Body of Christ, not through the priestly liturgy but through the mystery of the Holy Spirit. This view of the nature of eucharistic memory was a source of dissonance between Calvin and other Reformers like Ulrich Zwingli. Zwingli, echoing the perspective of some of his humanist training, felt that the scriptural account of the Last Supper suggested a symbolic equation of Christ's body with the bread. The Eucharist meal was for Zwingli, therefore, about the recollection of a story and amounted to a memorial meal. Eucharist was a symbolic act rather than an action with substantive transformative effect. Christ's presence in the meal or in the elements in themselves was, for Zwingli, symbolic rather than substantive.

At issue between the key thinkers of the Reformation was how Christ was present in the Eucharist itself. The question of Christ's presence was directly connected to the assumed efficacy of the sacrament. While few contemporary Christians live and die by these theological questions concerning the Eucharist, we are the heirs of the multifarious ethos that has been handed down around how the Eucharist is practiced and plays out. The contextual, embodied, race-conscious approach of this particular project invites a kind of scrutiny that leans less on revisiting these theological questions and engages more with actual human connection, context, and communal brokenness.

3. Ibid., 157ff.

4. Many theologians and liturgists understand Eucharistic anamnesis this way. Johann Baptist Metz is famous for his definition of this memory as "dangerous memory," which is about focusing on suffering, especial others' suffering, to connect us in solidarity with victims through narrative and to address that suffering in connection with God. Metz, *Love's Strategy*.

In order to meet the challenge of our task, which is to explore eucharistic memory and its wounding and healing realities in white-dominant faith communities, we need a framework of understanding for the ways that memory works and functions in human life and community. We need a shared understanding of body memory, trauma memory, social memory, and public memory. With this shared understanding we can explore the power and promise of counter-memory and "dangerous memory" for eucharistic practices that have a healing intention around race and privilege.

Our task is to investigate eucharistic memory and how it can connect a community to Jesus in such a way that that connection and that remembering can open up the contemporary situation and the challenges faced by those communities. More specifically, our challenge is to name how white-dominant communities employ eucharistic memory in modes that either heal or further wound when it comes to the realities of race and privilege. When is eucharistic memory simply nostalgic in these contexts, disregarding the complexity of memory? While all memory is selective, when is eucharistic memory narrowed and constrained by only acknowledging the parts of the memory that may appeal to individual needs rather than opening up our awareness of the social realities that challenge the status quo?

Body Memory and Trauma

Truly excavating the contours of eucharistic memory requires careful attention to the complexity of memory itself. All memory includes bodily memory. This fact means that memory is held deep in the body's physiology. This embodied complexity of memory has some very important characteristics for us to acknowledge. First, making room for the nature of body memory is not to be neatly equated with surfacing narratives that require taking the form of conscious memory in order to truly register as what "counts" as memory. Second, bodily memory is not to be mistaken with the need to release memories that have been repressed or forgotten.[5]

Bodily memory points us toward the infinite complexity of memory because it is always and already embedded in the tissues and cells of our bodies. Far from being simply a filing system in our brains, memory resides in sensation and, more mystifying still, in the cells and muscle twitches of our unconscious experience. We are actually conscious of a tiny percentage of our experience. Even though much of our embodied experience occurs underneath the radar of conscious thought, these unconscious and embodied experiences are deeply formative. They help to form us and to filter our conscious experiences and conscious memories as well.

Our embodied experience, therefore, creates an irreducible uniqueness in the ways each of us remembers and re-members the experiences and narratives that help shape who we are. This uniqueness is idiosyncratically in-formed by our context and our sense of self. Race, culture, economic situation, nutrition, parenting, environment, personality, laughter, community, and an infinite list of other things all play into how the body processes and re-members the inheritance of its unique experiences. Everything from writing and dreaming, to fear and shame, to simple physical experiences that never surface as emotion or sensation help shape how memories weave their way through our lives. Both conscious memories and the memories that our bodies hold of smells, tastes, feelings, love, harm, connection, and loneliness commingle with the cultural norms of behavior and understanding into which we have been habituated.

These shared norms of behavior that affect the flow and form of memory are tangled up with deeply ingrained bodily habituations. Edward Casey, Pierre Bourdieu, and other theorists of the body describe these susceptibilities of the body as "habitus" or "habitudes."[6] The body is a "matrix of nature and culture."[7] The

5. The dynamics of body memory are discussed in similar terms in Mount Shoop, *Let the Bones Dance*, 51.

6. Casey, "Ghost of Embodiment"; Bourdieu, *Outline of a Theory of Practice*.

7. Ibid., 214.

body is a "socially informed body" consisting of "a system of lasting, transposable dispositions which, integrating past experiences, functions at every moment as a matrix of perceptions, appreciations and actions."[8] As durable dispositions, pre-reflective bodily habituations shape behaviors that we do not always need to reflect upon—our skills such as playing tennis or swimming, our tastes, our likes and dislikes, and our culturally conditioned reactions to those who are "other."[9] Such bodily habituations embody cultural representations of groups and our pre-reflective body processes; what is designated as "the way to act" is conditioned by the shared worlds we occupy, our social networks, our family systems, our cultural contexts.

The ravages of trauma intersect with the complexity of memory in ways that need our attention here as well. The legacy of slavery and the history of racism are violent in their realities and in the ways they ripple through our bodies and our communities. Scholars are discovering again and again that trauma overrides the healthy, even though complex, formation of memory. Trauma induces an arrest, repetitive thoughts and visceral experiences, exaggerated habituations of vigilance and anxiety, and a heightened sense of foreboding and danger.

Post-traumatic stress syndrome (PTSD) is the medical diagnosis given to the body's telling ways of holding trauma. Hyper-vigilance, paranoia, sleep disturbances, nightmares, risky behavior, emotional numbness, disassociation, aggression, anger, and panic comprise just a part of the diagnostic profile for trauma survivors.[10] A vivid example of the ways in which trauma overrides the healthy flow and function of memory is clearly revealed in the mysterious world of dreams, an important and often unconscious way that our minds sort through experiences to create meaning. A

8. Bourdieu, *Outline of a Theory of Practice*, 16–17.

9. While these dispositions are characterized by a pre-reflective enactment, they can also be surfaced for scrutiny and relearning. Ibid. Connerton expands this concept to distinguish between habituations that occur in rituals, bodily technologies, and bodily proprieties. Connerton, *How Societies Remember*.

10. Mount Shoop, *Let the Bones Dance*, 42–43.

normal dream life includes deleting and sorting. "You'll feel better in the morning" is not just a turn of phrase but expresses the reality of how we create meaning and identity through the involuntary play of dreams. Traumatic dreams, however, do not follow this same pattern and process. Rather than helping us process feelings or experiences, trauma dreams seem to be purely repetitive and often re-traumatizing. These dreams involve a re-experiencing of trauma that does not help us "get to a better place" but instead continually take us back to a place where we are not safe. Such dreams can become life-diminishing. They do not respond to the same kinds of therapeutic processes that other dreams do. Flexibility of memory is one way practitioners and scholars explore as a healing modality in response to trauma. Inserting intention, beauty, safety, strength, or solace into the tenacity of trauma has been shown to create some malleability and movement toward healing.[11]

The distinctiveness of trauma dreams surfaces the dynamics of trauma for our bodies. Trauma takes up home-place in the body in ways that often arrest the healthy complexity of embodied experience. Sensations can be dulled, emotions on edge. Things like exaggerated startle reflexes, hypervigilance, flashbacks, and severe paranoia and depression can take hold. The body, like the trauma dreams, can live in an arrested, unsafe space in tenacious and harmful ways even when one's context no longer includes the traumatizing threat.

The embodied contours of trauma memory and body memory do not inhabit us as isolated individuals, but they help define our uniqueness in a complex web of connection and relationship. Our remembering and re-membering affect the ways we engage in community and the ways communities are shaped by our presence. Memory is not simply a dynamic of discrete bodies; it weaves through our lived social realities, creating shared stories, dissonance that we hold in secret, and transgressive spaces of narratives of resistance. The fact that social memory is reproduced through bodily habituations that are both unique and shared means that

11. Van der Kolk and van der Hart, "Intrusive Past," 178.

trauma that is shared or "cultural" in its scope, like racism and slavery, finds a home in communities and collectives.

The shared trauma of slavery, systemic racism, and racist attitudes and behavior has diminished human life for the entire human race, but black bodies have borne the brunt. This woundedness goes back generations, deep into the crevices of hearts, souls, and bodies beyond number. The harm is quantified by everything from the wealth and achievement gaps to limited access to housing and quality education. Underneath the surface are the ways black and brown bodies themselves embody the stress, strain, and woundedness of daily exposure to racism. Lower life expectancy, higher infant mortality rates, and a greater prevalence of heart disease, cancer, and diabetes for black and brown bodies surface the marks of racism's legacy. While conventional thinking may try to blame these differences in health outcomes on things like poverty and lifestyle choices, even when we correct for these factors statistically, the racialized disadvantage for black and brown bodies is still undeniable.[12] While the ravages of racism exact a cost on all of humanity, the price has been highest for black and brown bodies.

Cultural trauma can also habituate groups to take on shared dispositions and behaviors. For instance, some groups can be habituated to react with careful self-protective bodily postures when in contact with other groups. The cultural lessons that are instilled in young black men about the dangers that exist for them in the process of law enforcement embody this dynamic. For many whites, the shadow side of this hypervigilance for people of color is a deeply ingrained fear and tension around people of color, particularly young men of color. Cultural trauma habituates these responses along with the realities of oppression and abuse that continue today. Trauma continues to help shape reality and to be ingrained in how we navigate the world.

These same dynamics of memory that create both shared and transgressive narratives occupy space with unconscious muscle memories and body habituations formed in the service of memories we are not able to speak or name with words. These

12. Wise, *Colorblind*, 112–26.

unconscious narratives deeply affect and form the communities and relationships we inhabit. In its most life-giving incarnation, eucharistic memory is the template for how these complexities of memory can find community and redemptive capacity. Jesus modeled that redemptive possibility in his language of betrayal and redemption at the Last Supper. As we explore later in the chapter, this language of betrayal has been muted in telling ways in white-dominant faith communities. And with that silencing has come an arrested space when it comes to deep communal healing around race.

Social Memory, Public Memory, and Counter-Memory

Given the complex dynamics of bodies and trauma for memory, three categories help further frame how a "contemporary situation" is comprised of memory: *social memory*, *public memory*, and *counter-memory*. These categories enable us to consider how church populations are shaped by different kinds of memory. The category of *social memory* names the common, overlapping experiences that help construct group memories for individuals. Such memory comes into being through shared events and is reproduced through bodily habituations, community practices, shared narratives, and unconscious incorporations of both accepted meanings and transgressive interpretations of the events. The power dimensions of social reality mean that there will always be some versions of shared memories that dominate the public realm. This *public memory* inevitably impacts all social groups regardless of whether they agree with the public version. At the same time there are accounts that may function as *counter-memory* that are hidden and often go unacknowledged by groups with the most power. Given the variable effects of the racialized past of American culture on different groups, including denial and obliviousness as well as what W. E. B. Du Bois called "double-consciousness," there is serious demand for acknowledgment of the variety of ways in which social memory, especially traumatic social memory, shapes different groups. Further unpacking the categories for social memory in light of these complexities will help us explore social memory in eucharistic practice.

A common way of defining social memory is the public memory displayed in what counts as the official national versions of U.S. history, represented in monuments, national holidays, media representations, and required history books. Even with these examples of shared public memory, as noted, there are always different versions of this national memory that reflect different group experiences. The versions can vary greatly and typically include experiences not recognized in the official versions. For example, some First Nation peoples or Native Americans argue that the very invention of this public narrative is a colonial practice created to invisibilize them as a people, a virtual "logic of genocide."[13] This dynamic is similarly at work in the invisibilizing that continues around the legacy of the enslavement of black people in this country. Social memory differs for a variety of groups because they have had radically different experiences of what can appear to be the same reality.

These differences are important and pronounced when we account for power differentials between the dominant racial group and groups who have been systematically oppressed. The systemic power differences clearly translate into stark discrepancies when it comes to how social memory is represented in the public realm. As indicated earlier such memory includes material culture and embodied memory, not just symbols and narratives. The effects of the trauma of slavery and ongoing racist practices can be seen over time not simply in African Americans' learned distrust of whites but also in bodily habituations of things like deference around whites with lessons like "don't look a white man in the eye." These bodily habituations can also shape-shift according to context, revealing one version of the self in white company—what Du Bois called "double-consciousness," wherein blacks learn to be aware of the white world as something distinct from their own. Such habituations do not have to be consciously reflected upon and then enacted; they become "natural" ways of surviving. As trauma

13. Smith, "First Nation, Empire, and Globalization," 308.

arrests the body in a state of hypervigilance, social trauma can create tenacious shared norms for survival in a racialized world.

Traumatic social memory thus surfaces the creation of a *social identity*, the resulting shared *group memory*, and the way in which a *counter-memory* can emerge. Social identity generally develops from shared experiences significant enough to create a culturally dispersed sense of "we." This "we" is also informed by the prevalent ways that groups are marked or categorized by the dominant culture. Another layer of tenacity emerges when the group can create a shared narrative. Because of the common ways people of color have been marked by American society and have experienced many things in American society, a discernible and powerful social identity generated by shared oppression and trauma has clearly emerged over time. Cultural trauma entails loss and "a tear in the social fabric," which can create "a membership group as it identifies an event or an experience, a primal scene, that solidifies individual/collective identity."[14]

Slavery was that "primal scene" which could unite black and brown people whether they experienced it or not.[15] While a variety of social markers and connections can bring groups of whites together, including traumatic experiences, the creation of a social identity claimed or assumed by *all* whites is less clear, given the prominence of white domination.[16] The white perception of ourselves as not having "race" and as having the power to define other

14. "As opposed to psychological or physical trauma, which involves a wound and the experience of great emotional anguish by an individual, cultural trauma refers to a dramatic loss of identity and meaning, a tear in the social fabric affecting a group of people that has achieved some degree of cohesion." Eyerman, *Cultural Trauma*, 2.

15. Ibid., 2, 14f., 1. This is not to make a reductive claim about what connects African Americans; there is clearly much diversity among persons of color beyond this reality. Slavery and extended racism are, however, a shared marker of the past.

16. Oppression relative to identity markers of class, gender, and sexual orientation can bring some whites together around a shared and traumatized identity. There are also "counter-memories" that are generated by these groups, such as women's histories. The point here is that there seems to be no marker that characterizes all whites.

groups as having ethnicity and race has authorized those of us who are white to understand ourselves as the ostensibly "normal" human beings. Although this aspect of colorblindness is clearly a position of privilege and thus, in some sense, a form of social identity, it is not a "marked" identity. This distinction allows whites to designate other group's identities by their racial and ethnic markers.

When it comes to the resulting shared memory that connects a group to that social identity, there are clear differences between those marked in American culture as black or African American and those who identify as white. African American corporate identity was profoundly generated by slavery and has long included very different readings of American white history. While complicated and expanded by post-slavery (and Jim Crow) history, African American social memory continues to include this traumatic historical past. In contrast, the more vague white social identity seems to generate acceptance of a supposedly "objective," unmarked memory as has been displayed in national history, long defined by those with power.

Thus "counter-memory" differs for these groups as well. For African Americans, as well as other oppressed groups, counter-memory to the dominant "objective" national history has been necessary; it has resisted the invisibilizing of African American agency and diversity and attempted to publicize white racism in its complexity. And in our current times, history that does attend to racialization is expanding more and more from popular media into classrooms and textbooks. Any nascent shared white counter-memory, however, does not intentionally attend to recovery and narration of that racialized past. White hypocrisy, dehumanizing racism, quiet assent to racist systems, and even the perceived generosity of missionary approaches of the past have been acknowledged and even reformed of some of their paternalism and condescension.[17] A shared white "counter-memory," however, is too often about sustaining the dominant view and countering

---

17. Wilmore, *Black and Presbyterian*, 32, 42f. In his brief review of white complicity in slavery and other racism, Wilmore reveals the particularly negative actions of Presbyterians compared to several other denominations.

alternatives.[18] As race issues of the past get more public attention, white denial and dismissal are common. The civil rights movement "helped transform the cultural trauma of a group into a national trauma. Since then and only since then has slavery become part of America's collective memory." However, even with the shared and relatively contemporary experience and images and public memory of the civil rights movement, there has been no "white response" or development of counter-memory to broadly acknowledge how whites have benefited and continue to benefit from the systems and institutions that racism helped form. And white denial continues to resist shared responsibility for these problems.[19]

Eucharistic Memory and Dangerous Memory

The prominence of white power profoundly affects these categories of memory, and an examination of Christian churches will not find much difference. Most mainline, white-derived denominations remain predominantly white. Even as racism is acknowledged in the Presbyterian Church (U.S.A.), Gayraud Wilmore argues that the middle-class status of most black Presbyterians has contributed to a "confused identity" where there seems to be more accommodation to white culture and less claiming of black history in black churches.[20] He also calls upon the need to address "Whitenization," which amounts to "accommodation to the color-blindness and ethnic neutrality that is a game White Presbyterians sometimes play."[21] This dynamic suggests the idiosyncratic way that different people and communities embody the narratives and counter-narratives of race in particular contexts.

18. There are growing numbers of exceptions, including the focus on anti-racism trainings. Tim Wise has written numerous books on whiteness. Other examples are Frankenberg, *Displacing Whiteness;* Brown et al., *Whitewashing Race.*

19. Eyerman, *Cultural Trauma,* 17–18.

20. Wilmore, *Black and Presbyterian,* 53, 60, 65–71.

21. Ibid., 67.

Eucharist can be normatively envisioned in communities that set their intention on substantive healing around racialized woundedness. Eucharistic memory has the capacity to be a different kind of memory that intersects with our human and social identities and memories. Eucharistic memory can embody and practice "dangerous memory." This kind of transformative and transgressive memory is the kind of remembering that Jesus modeled in his life, death, and resurrection. It is the kind of memory he invited in his Last Supper. This transformative and transgressive memory is intended to open up and address the concreteness and brokenness of our contemporary situation. And exploring the contours of dangerous memory can help us notice how eucharistic memory is not functioning in this transformative and transgressive mode when it comes to the racialized realities of white-dominant churches.

"Dangerous memory," a phrase invoked by theologian Johann Baptist Metz, is intended to disrupt the self-protective and banal ways that the Christian tradition can be deployed. Dangerous memory disrupts practices of meaning that simply repeat biblical passages or constrain the reach of faith by making it "safe" for those who wish to keep the status quo. Dangerous memory follows Jesus as the "dangerous Christ" into solidarity with those who have been harmed by the powerful.[22] Jesus' solidarity with the oppressed was and is about liberation from suffering and oppression. Jesus' ministry was about transformation. And the "dangerous Christ" continues the work of the biblical God who acts in history to liberate the captive. This God of the oppressed is and always will be "allied" with the weak, from the "insignificant tribes of Israel to . . . the defeated Jesus of Nazareth on the cross."[23]

This memory is disruptive and dangerous because it attends to God's presence with the suffering of the world. This dangerous memory is "interruptive" of the contemporary situation and its reading of history. When engaged in a mode of dangerous remembering, we cannot forget or deny past suffering or the

22. Metz, *Love's Strategy*, 77.
23. Ibid., 80.

abuses of power that create systems of oppression: "History, as a remembered history of suffering, acquires for reason the form of a 'dangerous tradition,' which is passed on not in a purely argumentative manner, but as narrative, that is, in 'dangerous stories.'"[24] Dangerous memory and its stories compel us to follow God in and through solidarity with those who have been most deeply harmed.[25] Dangerous memory invites us to testify to the ways we have been harmed as well.

Attention to dangerous memory resurfaces and accentuates our collective need to recognize context and location. While there is a "public memory" of Christianity and a social group identity for Christian communities of faith, these are not definable as simply "Christian." In other words, while there is a history of Christianity in the same way that there is a history of the U.S. (i.e., a public memory), being "Christian" is not the same as having "U.S. citizen" as our social identity. Prominent theological trajectories portray the church as defined in contrast to, over against, or even transformative of the world. Ideally, being "Christian" should not be reducible to the cultural, institutional elements of a nation, a club, or an organization. This is not to say that culture, race, class, nationality, and other markers of group identity don't exist for faith communities; indeed, they are part of being human. However, that they always already shape our judgments and practices in ways that can blind us to groups considered "other" is rarely acknowledged by white communities. Acknowledging these realities is a first step in the transformative and dangerous work to which the church is called.

Our description of white Presbyterian eucharistic liturgy and its docile, careful performance is an example. It is not simply biblical or Christian or Reformed but is shaped by cultures that are intertwined with Presbyterianism and its complicated history. Most importantly, this unavoidable reality must be continually examined for its possibilities, including how it may be functioning

24. Ibid., 111.

25. Metz's work on these categories is extensive. The references here are only a few examples.

to blind us to other realities. How have white-dominant ecclesiological memories and narratives been remembered and embodied? Can we collectively surface the blindness and prejudice of our institutional past? What about our faith identity can surface and disrupt the harmful refusal of white-dominant institutions to acknowledge their being shaped by culture? The paradox of Christian identity in our contemporary moment holds the tension that while we cannot live our faith without cultural, social, and contextual particularity, these layers of our identity and memory can become harmful when we are blind to their reality and reification.

To explore eucharistic memory in a way that takes whiteness, white denial, and power seriously, the unacknowledged "public memory" of Christianity needs to be foregrounded by a "counter-memory" that attends to racialized suffering and how to address it. In short, the ways in which our "official" version of the right way to be Christian dominates need to be surfaced, named, and critically examined. This constructive framework also requires attention to the processes of identity formation for Christians that could give rise to a Christian *collective identity*, an identity that takes concrete social realities seriously. This collective identity needs to ask how social markers contribute to and also hinder and blind us to racialized wounding and potential transformative practices. How can attention to and creation of counter-memory as dangerous memory inform a white Christian collective identity that can function as a liberating and transforming counter-memory to colorblindness? Attention to the main narratives of Jesus suggests how eucharistic memory might be dangerous rather than docile.

Re-membering the Dangerous Christ

Jesus was an outlier. And in the end he was betrayed and forsaken by his own disciples and violently put to death by his community. In our celebration of Eucharist, Jesus invites us to display and practice a life of truth in the face of violence and of power-sharing in the face of domination. Being keenly aware of the power dynamics that constituted his world, from betrayal and violence to lies and power, Jesus identified with the "least of these" and aligned himself not with dominance but with the deep woundedness of our condition. He was on the losing side of human power differentials. He suffered at the hands of some of his most trusted friends, and suffered with those on the margins of his community of faith. And faith, community, friendship, and power are what Jesus sought to transform with the way he connected. Even with the violence and betrayal of his last days, he shape-shifted these realities into a healing opportunity.

This counter-memory of Jesus challenges typical contemporary eucharistic practices. Such a Jesus does not portray a paradigm for reified liturgy but for a radical flexibility and responsiveness. Even as the primary images of Jesus in liturgy include reference to a body broken for us and blood poured out for us in a sacrificial act of love, accounts of our contemporary situations and their brokenness are rarely entangled with how the power, betrayal, and dis-memberment of a man by his community surfaces a dangerous narrative for those with power. Rituals can often become "disconnected" from our lives, sometimes because the primary focus is simply to repeat them as "*the* tradition." Stories of contemporary lives and their brokenness often do not appear in the liturgy.[26] And these well-worn habits create eucharistic habituations for many white churches that are not dangerous in the ways Jesus is remembered. This "safe" remembering is unable to surface the social brokenness that "dangerous memory" would invite us to address.[27]

Christians, in our zeal to make the cross the final expiation for our sin, have generally "whitewashed" the power of the cross to

26. As Anderson and Foley argue, "A basic difficulty with Sunday Eucharist is not that it is poor theater but that it is poor human storytelling and inadequate storytelling. While a solemn, well-planned Lord's Supper may proclaim loudly the great divine narrative, it often fails to make connections with the real stories of people's ordinary lives." *Mighty Stories, Dangerous Rituals*, x, 128f., 152. See also Grimes, *Reading, Writing, and Ritualizing*.

27. This is not to say the topics do not come up anywhere in a worship service. A sermon or list of shared "community concerns" can include reference to forms of social brokenness, and biblical passages that invoke God's call for justice can be read. It is significant, however, that liturgy does not typically foreground contemporary forms of social brokenness.

bear the sins of the world for us to see them more clearly. The cross offers an icon of the blindness of domination and the tenacity of denial. Jesus uses this space of betrayal to surface disruptive and challenging realities. Can this reality of his death break through the tenacious layers of white denial to cultivate a dangerous memory for white-dominated churches? The chronic reenactments of our social "not-knowing" and our captivity to denial mask the ongoing effects of racism. The rupture of relationships and community calls out for the dissonant fragments to be heard, to be re-membered. The genius of the body's capacity for regeneration in the wake of trauma invites us to explore how the Body of Christ might likewise experience a deep healing from the flexibility that imagination and dangerous memory offer us.

Trauma complicates the possibilities and pathways of healing in our liturgical practices because traumatic memory is characterized by pure repetition, not by processional transformation. Dis-membered eucharistic practice thus becomes a serial re-traumatizing of communities cut off from one another because it is virtual repetition; it fails to surface the hidden realities of implicit bias and does not effect change. The experiences of these repetitions are always unique and particular to the cultural contexts and experiences that inform communities and individuals, even as they all participate in this shared repetitive dynamic. Despite real changes in laws, ideals, and aspirations, our habits continue to embody deeply embedded harm. We whites continue to think only "explicit" prejudiced bias matters, even as our ongoing lived practices with persons of our own racial group leave implicit stereotypical views of the "other" unchanged. In white culture the "colorblind" story we tell ourselves and the prominence of what Bonilla-Silva calls our "white habitus" embody our profound denial and our repetitive dis-membering habits of community formation.

Flexibility requires a knowledge and awareness of the depth of the harm that exists. This acknowledgment and awareness is more about an assent to the reality of the depth of harm than it is about being able to access it all and bring it up into a conscious, discrete narrative. Flexibility also requires relational connection where there is room to abide in the repetitive return that trauma entails. This supportive environment helps create the conditions of possibility for communal skills to develop around noticing the cycles of repetition and denial, without judgment and blame. Flexibility also requires a mode of playful and experimental generation of language and practice. Just as believers dance around the edges of God's mystery with our liturgies and language about the Divine, so do our sacramental sensitivities and practices need to be malleable enough to respond to the ebb and flow of new insight, new connection, and new imagination.

five

Re-membering Eucharist

Embodied flexibility (a working definition): susceptibil-
ity to modification and adaptation; willingness and/or
disposition of pliability and response-ability.[1]

Colorblindness denies the wounds of race. Having the eyes
to notice and acknowledge our true colors enables a sacred
flexibility that rests not in blame and shame but in the desire to
re-member the Body of Christ, that Body which has been dismembered by betrayal, ruptured by fear, and punctured by abuses of
power. Jesus' naming of betrayal at his Last Supper was his dangerous way of calling out our deepest affliction with healing in
mind. And he would have the wounds to show for it—as do we.
But far from staying in the annihilating repetition and isolation
that trauma induces, Jesus calls us toward healing opportunities in
our life together.

The genius of the body's capacity for regeneration in the wake
of trauma gives us clues to how the Body of Christ might likewise habituate a communal healing intention through practices of
flexibility and imagination in the gathered Body. Our hope is that
exploring and embodying practices of eucharistic flexibility can
shake loose some of the repetitive behaviors that reify racialized
harm and that we can begin to feed our collective imagination

1. The practice and disposition of response-ability is discussed in Mount
Shoop, *Let the Bones Dance*, 65–91.

with new, life-giving sensations and experiences. This invitation to flexibility continues to find embodied expression in contexts and in real bodies. And so, eucharistic flexibility invites and requires experimentation and exploration in communities and contexts beyond this project and the particular experiences of the authors of this book.

Exploring the redemptive and healing capacity of flexibility in eucharistic practices in the wake of the social trauma of racism is deep and delicate work, and it is nothing if not embodied. Intellectual curiosity with and rhetorical ascent to flexibility are not what eucharistic practice requires for its transformative capacity to have space to breathe. While practicing flexibility can be greatly enhanced by the conscious acknowledgment of the complexity and depth of harm, its most primary invitation is the willingness to suspend the need to completely understand or perfectly describe that harm. This acknowledgment and awareness must commingle with embodied practices of incompetency, connection, and shared power in white-dominant contexts.

Practicing these skills helps create the conditions necessary for generosity to be extended to dissonant voices and experiences. From practicing incompetency (e.g., practices that release us from the burden of always being right, of there being a "right" way to do things, of always being "good" at what we do) comes a mode of playful and experimental generation of language, practice, and exploration. From practicing connection (e.g., practices that bring us into proximity with others, practices that embody our deep connection with all that is) comes habituation of listening, truth-telling, and holding dissonant narratives gently. From practicing power-sharing (e.g., practices that honor different modes of exercising personal power, practices that clear space for all voices to be heard) comes the opportunity for communal skills to emerge around noticing and naming the systems and habits we oftentimes fail to acknowledge, skills that mirror the way Jesus named these layers of community at the Last Supper. These practices help us develop skills around dissonance and connection that allow us to notice, without judgment or blame, the repetitive ways we reify

racialized harm in many of the well-worn habits of white-dominant faith communities.

The following vignettes give us an opportunity to notice practices that can coax malleability out of our sacramental rigidity and
obliviousness. We may also notice how flexibility can stretch out
into new imaginations in particular contexts. How can the skills
needed in contexts of privilege to address the wounds of race with
a healing intention help cultivate communal capacities that are
generative of healing relationships and cultural change? This question can only be answered in context.

Three Vignettes of Flexibility

Practices of Incompetency, Idiosyncrasy, and Improvisation

Tuesday nights were a chance to sing, to be quiet in God's mysterious presence, and to meet around the Lord's Table for communion. We gathered in a formal, pristine sanctuary that was
routinely filled to the brim on Sundays.[2] Unlike Sundays, these
Tuesday gatherings were informal, only loosely scripted by a common rhythm of song, silence, and sacrament, and populated not
by hundreds but by tens and twenties. There was no printed order
of worship, no Elders appointed to serve communion in the pews,
no *Book of Common Worship* to read from for the liturgy, and no
sterling silver service.

We moved to the Table idiosyncratically, prompted by words,
by gestures, by a gentle touch, or by a song. And each week, we
celebrated that communion meal with attention to the real bodies
that were there. We looked each other in the eye, we served each
other side by side with words, touch, and acknowledgment. We
often shared our thanksgivings, our brushes with God, our hopes
and our needs around the Table with each other. Every week was
different, even as its content filled up the common rhythm of our
gatherings.

2. Marcia Mount Shoop facilitated these "Deep and Wide" worship services in a church in Chapel Hill, North Carolina.

Sometimes our communion was completely silent. Sometimes it included a time of sharing and talking to each other during the Great Thanksgiving. Sometimes our communion was simply a story and our wondering before we re-membered it again in our time around the Table. The very choreography of our gathering embodied dissonance in that space; our attempts to be fluid and to try new things had to work around pews bolted to the ground and a Table that took a work order to move.

Our openness to the mystery of the Table and the transformative power of the Table was practiced in multilayered ways. In our extended silence before communion (often twenty minutes) we practiced surrendering, quieting our minds, receiving instead of grasping, vulnerability, and breathing in the possibility of transformation. We learned new songs and we tried different genres of music. We chanted and we sang hymns. We listened to the hammer dulcimer, bluegrass, gospel, and contemporary Christian music played by a variety of people from the extended community.

All of these practices helped us learn new skills around the table: skills of flexibility, noticing, incompetency, trust, disorientation, and connection. We did not talk our way through these practices but explored them most often in the way we navigated the space, the community, and the meal itself with our bodies, our breath, our facial expressions, our tensions, and our sensations of grace and possibility.

Practices of Connecting, Re-membering, and Holding Dissonance

Eucharistic flexibility invites connection, re-membering, and holding dissonant narratives gently. And such communal flexibility can be practiced through extra-eucharistic practices that help shape-shift and modify communities in response to the realities of racialized woundedness and shared healing intentions.

A five-year-long church gathering called the "Pauli Murray Reading Group" emerged around a public project in North Carolina that employed the story of an African American woman activist as a "dangerous memory" to draw public attention to contemporary forms of racism, sexism, and heterosexism. A radical activist whose ancestors included a slave in Chapel Hill raped by the white slave owner, Pauli Murray grew up in Durham, North Carolina. She worked for civil rights in the 1960s and was a cofounder of the National Organization for Women (NOW) in 1966. She left NOW when she realized that "race" was not on their agenda and later became a lawyer. Her book *States' Laws on Race and Color* (1957) was called the Bible for the legal fight to end the "separate but equal" doctrine by chief counsel of the NAACP Thurgood Marshall.[3] Murray invented the term "Jane Crow." She went to divinity school in the 1970s and was ordained, becoming the first African American female Episcopal priest.

While not explicitly eucharistic, the church reading group uses Reverend Murray's story to surface participants' histories. We use her stories about her family, the role of racism and sexism in her life, and her struggles for justice to share our own stories about race, gender, and sexuality.[4] We ask ourselves questions: When did we first become aware of the category of race? When did we first become aware of the categories of gender and sexuality? We wonder together about how these "markers" have been oppressive or liberative in our lives. We also ask, how has our Christian faith mattered?

In exploring when we each became aware of race, we wrote letters to each other about what came up for us in this question. Eugene is an African American man in his fifties who grew up in rural North Carolina. He wrote,

> As a child in the late fifties and early sixties, I was isolated from white culture. I lived in a black community and since I was young did not interact with whites. My school was in the black community and all my teachers were black. This is not to say that I did not go where I saw whites. I was always in the protective context of family or

3. Murray, *Pauli Murray*, 289.

4. Mary McClintock Fulkerson is a member of the Pauli Murray Reading Group in Durham, North Carolina.

friend groups and did not interact with whites on a social level. There were two sets of bathrooms, two sets of water fountains, and there were places that I wasn't allowed to go. These were understood limits I did not question but accepted because my culture accepted them. My family wasn't into activism and did not preach social justice. We got a TV in about 1965 when I was around eleven years old, so up to that time I wasn't inundated with the black struggle. In 1970, I began going to an integrated high school. About this same time I came to the conclusion that all the law changes, forced integration, and extended education would not change the hearts of people. I saw that even the most progressive whites had a deep belief in their superiority. I saw in the smartest blacks a deep-seated question of how they could ever be good enough. How do you change an attitude forged over centuries? Some problems are the stuff of the church.

Another member of the group, Mary, who grew up in Mississippi, shared the following:

My family included three sisters and two brothers. We all grew up on my father's farm. Our main crop was cotton and corn. My father also owned a small dairy. I was educated in Mississippi. I graduated from Mississippi Valley State in 1968. My first experience with another race was while attending elementary school. My seventh-grade teacher decided to teach some of the students typing. We ordered six Royal manual typewriters. I was one of the students taking the class. We had a visit from the superintendent of schools and were told that we had to get rid of the typewriters. The superintendent asked the teacher, "Why are you teaching typing and shorthand to these students? They will never be able to use it." He said it was a waste of time. So, we had to send the typewriters back to the company. This experience still resonates with me today as I think of all the inequality that we had to endure because of our race.

As a white member of the group who grew up in Little Rock, Arkansas, I shared this reflection:[5]

> I grew up in a middle-class family that always went to a Presbyterian church. Indeed, while never overtly pious, my parents were very active in the Presbyterian churches we belonged to as we moved around the South. They raised me to be "responsible," ethical/moral, and, while less frequently named, to be a typical white middle-class girl who would probably grow up to be a caring mother who occupied (and did the unpaid labor of) the domestic sphere. My mother was just such a model and did lots of volunteer work at church, especially with the group known as Presbyterian Women. . . . What is most remarkable to me now about my years growing up in the South is my ignorance of and obliviousness to the issues, protests and historic events around race that were so prominent in the early years of my generation. While the 1954 *Brown v. Board of Education* Supreme Court decision to outlaw school segregation happened when I was four years old, what is most shocking is that the desegregation crisis at Central High School in 1957 happened in my city of birth—Little Rock. Although my family had moved to Texas by then, I was still completely unaware of these events. If they ever talked about them, I certainly didn't hear it.

When naming how we locate our awareness of race, participants told dissonant stories of obliviousness and awareness. Eugene described his growing awareness this way:

> So when did I really know racism? It is obvious that I lived it unknowingly all my life, but when did I look and ask, "What the f___ is going on here?" I am not very intuitive, but there came a time when I started interpreting these social truisms for myself. By the mid-1960s the voice of protest had become strong enough that even I began to hear and understand many things. I began to read and study the works of activists and historical

5. The "I" here refers to Mary McClintock Fulkerson who, as indicated, has been a part of the Pauli Murray Reading Group since it began.

leaders. In their description of structural racism I began to reassess my environment. I was as angry with myself as I was with racism. How could I not have seen this? The history of slavery and white-on-black hate crime consumed me during this time. I read everything I could get on black injustice. . . . I was around eleven or twelve when I experienced this awaking of who and what I was within the context of a repressive society. I began understanding its sinister nature that makes you part of its practices. . . . As hatred consumed me, it took a much older book to save me.

Mary described her way of dealing with this painful reality:

With God's help, I have worked my way through some of the bitterness. I was very blessed to be born into a very supportive family. We were taught never to allow anyone to define who you are. I was blessed to have such a caring and supportive community. Thanks for allowing me to share this experience. Of course, there are many other incidents that I could share, but decided to only share the one that is still a part of me today.

I described mine this way:

The kind of racial awareness that I had growing up is emblematic of the worldview of countless Southern privileged whites, especially of my generation. The only blacks I knew were our maids, the African American women who cleaned our houses and, especially, the house of my paternal grandparents. . . . Given our moving around so much, their home was a place of stability and for celebrating holidays. Their maid, Roberta, stands out most clearly in my memory. She was so kind and caring to us and worked for them for years. (Seeing *The Help* is gaggy and embarrassing.) . . . My first "awareness" was that of a white person who grows up assuming that blacks were a different kind of people—people who "work" for us, but that's about all. Only in my later years as an academic did my interest in feminist theology generate my (academic) interest in other marginalized groups besides "women." So race became a crucial category along with gender. It was only when I did a study of an interracial church that I began to have more experiential awareness of different experiences—especially as I saw how "nice" Christians (like me) could be supposedly well-meaning and yet so profoundly oblivious to the cost of racism and unacknowledged white privilege.

Such honesty cultivates communal practices resonating with eucharistic practice. Different bodies come together as our faith invokes an honest re-membering of past oppression and complicity. While there will never be a way to "fix" the harm of racial and other forms of social trauma that have shaped us, the Pauli Murray gatherings create the possibility for naming our wounds and for healing opportunities that come along with such honest connections. With people of different races telling their stories, the substantive and honest connections that white obliviousness has blocked for centuries are now beginning to happen.

Practices of Power-Sharing, Solidarity, and Truth-Telling

In the summer of 2014 disparate groups, ministers, and local citizens in North Carolina came together outside the state legislative building in Raleigh to enact (embody) our concern for the social good. This gathering named the refusal of many lawmakers to hear the concerns of North Carolina's most vulnerable people. Some of the specific social issues this gathering addressed included access to health care being put at risk with the denial of Medicaid expansion, the concern of working people over their loss of earned income tax credits, risks to full democracy due to the denial of voting rights to the vulnerable, and the harm to public education in the reduction of pay for public teachers and reduction of teacher assistants. This was not an ordinary protest. We communicated these concerns through a public ritual in the form of a justice-focused communion.[6] This communal practice invoked liberative memory in a broadly diverse community gathered in order to

6. Mary McClintock Fulkerson participated in this gathering in Raleigh, North Carolina.

address specific forms of contemporary brokenness. All brought bread to share in a liturgy of solidarity and protest.[7] Aspects of the words we spoke together surface the practices and intention of this gathering.

The prayer included language naming our common purpose and the betrayal of the community. This language echoes the truth-telling Jesus did at the Last Supper around friendship and betrayal. Here are some excerpts of the prayer:

> Creator God,
> We thank Thee for giving us the gift of life.
> We thank Thee for giving us the gift of love.
> We thank Thee for giving us the gift of beloved community.
> God, we are one people, sisters and brothers in one family. . . .
> Black, white and brown,
> We stand together to continue
> the fight for life,
> for love,
> and for beloved community.
>
> We remember how, when you brought the people out of Egypt,
> you fed them with bread from heaven;
> and no one among them was in need.
>
> **Let us break bread together, marching on.**
> **Let's all say together: Let us break bread together, marching on (2x)**
>
> We remember how in the Christian tradition,
> you blessed two fish and five loaves of bread,
> and five thousand hungry souls were fed.
>
> **Let us break bread together, marching on!**

---

7. The communion liturgy was distributed in written form to the crowd with no author listed.

We remember how in Islam, we cannot celebrate
the *Eid* until each person has offered charity to the hungry.

Let us break bread together, marching on.

We are gathered together today to celebrate a love feast
with all those who will commit to your way
of mercy and compassion.
We are deeply concerned by the extreme policies passed by our
general assembly last year,
and by their refusal to hear the cries of North Carolina's most
vulnerable.

We remember the African proverb that says, "He who cannot
hear the mouth eating, cannot hear the mouth crying."
We know we cannot feel one another's pain unless we break
bread together.

Let us break bread together, marching on.

We invite the honorable members of this legislative body who
will stand with this Moral Movement to join us for this love
feast. . . .

Let us break bread together, marching on. . . .

People with vastly different and even dissonant social loca-
tions and identities shared bread with strangers who shared a passion for the common good. This gathering walked quietly into the
capitol building, through the main building, up the stairs, and then
outside the back entrance, singing as we went. We then gathered
together outside to share our commitments and hope.[8]

8. The leader, Rev. Dr. William Barber, on the board of the NAACP, pastor
of Greenleaf Disciples of Christ Church in Goldsboro, North Carolina, has
continued to work for social justice in North Carolina, including the sponsor-
ing of "Moral Mondays" throughout the state.

From Colorblind to True Colors

Practices of flexibility embodied in these particular contexts give us glimpses and glimmers of how Eucharist can be a template for healing opportunities around the wounds of race. Practices of incompetency, idiosyncrasy, and improvisation give us glimpses of the capacity of our embodied habituations to find new patterns and possibilities. Practices of connecting and holding dissonance are windows into the healing capacity of substantive face-to-face interactions honest about the wounds of race. And practices of power-sharing and truth-telling at the eucharistic table broadly construed open up possibilities for structural and cultural shifts in life-giving directions.

All three vignettes give us glimpses of stretching and malleability in contexts of faith. Re-membering that is explicit, honest, and dissonant is rare in faith communities, especially white-dominant faith communities. These same communities struggle with change and being playful or adventuresome with liturgy or eucharistic practice. And allowing social memory to be articulated for the purpose of opening up the brokenness of our contemporary lives is likewise not a common exercise in white-dominant churches.

The flexibility and generativity of Eucharist embodies the capacity to connect and even to heal in the face of profound communal woundedness. This capacity is more than just giving voice to generic confession from official liturgies—for example, "Merciful God, we confess that we have sinned against you in thought, word, and deed, by what we have done, and by what we have left undone. We have not loved you with our whole heart and mind and strength. We have not loved our neighbors as ourselves."[9] While we may find it easy to recite the confession, the ripple effects of shared trauma like racism take up a home-place in our deepest habits and reflexes and are not necessarily recognized by our ritual recitations. These shared contortions and diminishments can create communal stasis and inflexibility. Like unused muscles,

9. Presbyterian Church (U.S.A.), *Book of Common Worship*, 53.

communities that become routinized in sameness and denial can atrophy and become rigid.

Even as we confess sin regularly, violent legacies like the ones we all inherit from slavery, racism, and privilege mark us far beneath our capacity to see ourselves as both those who harm and those who are harmed by these deep-seated reverberations of ruptured relationships. The marks are held in our habituations, in our instincts, in our stiffened bodies, in our unconscious biases, and in our postures and gestures. And these habituations and postures are even more tenacious when we do not acknowledge the depth of harm that has been done. At its best Eucharist invites a way to embody awareness of that harm.

Flexibility is nurtured with robust theological and existential imagination as well as through acknowledgment of our embodied habituations and capacity for transformation. For whites new imaginations can create the conditions of possibility necessary for facing the realities of racism honestly. This honest acknowledgment avoids both superficial "reconciliation" and Manichean accounts of "good guys vs. bad guys" in black-white relations. Remembering our broken relationships and ruptured communities around race and privilege is a process that necessarily involves change and also a redefining of relationships. The healing of relationships is also more than simply a cognitive transition; it is an embodied one.[10] The process of change and redefinition requires a period of transition. Change is one thing (laws that make segregation illegal), but for whites to fully take in and recognize the wounds of race will require transition to a new worldview. This worldview is something that is more time-consuming than "change" and is a significant alternative to the "fix" of colorblindness. Avoidance

---

10. It is important to distinguish between a "reconciliation paradigm," which is mostly concerned with relationships, and a paradigm of "reparations," which is concerned with the larger structures that support and re-create racial injustice, including attention to "white privilege." For attention to these issues, see Jennifer Harvey, *Dear White Christians*. Our project is only a start at fleshing out whiteness and its privilege, via attention to white colorblindness in church.

and denial give way to noticing, acknowledging, connecting, and re-membering.

Eucharist is a template for surfacing how this avoidance and denial has reified racialized harm. And Eucharist is a template for how flexibility and imagination can create new possibilities for healing from the wounds of race. While black and brown bodies bear the brunt of racism's wounds, white bodies laid bare also surface the effects of these wounds in the trivialization and diminishment that our communities embody. White bodies have benefited from racism at the same time they have been stunted by it. Our faith communities bear these marks of triviality and diminishing returns. And our Eucharistic practices embody these realities in the whitewashed ways we deny that there is a problem.

Eucharist, in its fullest flower, holds together and embodies the tension between deep love and devotion and the pain of betrayal and broken community. Eucharistic practices are trivialized when we fail to re-member how Jesus invites his beloved to stay close to him at the same time he names the breach and the harm that is at work in that same space of fellowship and friendship. Embodying attention and acknowledgment of this conflicted space that Jesus occupied with his community requires the conscious overlay of race and privilege if we are truly open to the transformation in our current cultural context. And may these wounds find healing opportunities in communities gathered with such sacred intention.

Bibliography

Alexander, Jeffrey C. *Trauma: A Social Theory*. Cambridge: Polity, 2012.

Anderson, Herbert, and Edward Foley. *Mighty Stories, Dangerous Rituals: Weaving Together the Human and the Divine*. San Francisco: Jossey-Bass, 1998.

Baldovin, John F. "An Embodied Eucharistic Prayer." In *The Postures of the Assembly during the Eucharistic Prayer*, by John K. Leonard and Nathan D. Mitchell, 1–13. Chicago: Liturgy Training Publications, 1994.

Berger, Teresa. *Gender Differences and the Making of Liturgical History: Lifting a Veil on Liturgy's Past*. Burlington, VT: Ashgate, 2011.

Bieler, Andrea, and Luise Schottroff. *The Eucharist: Bodies, Bread, and Resurrection*. Minneapolis: Fortress, 2007.

Bonilla-Silva, Eduardo. *Racism without Racists: Color-Blind Racism and the Persistence of Racial Inequality in the United States*. 3rd ed. Lanham, MD: Rowman & Littlefield, 2010.

———. *White Supremacy and Racism in the Post-Civil Rights Era*. Boulder, CO: Lynne Rienner, 2001.

Bourdieu, Pierre. *Outline of a Theory of Practice*. Translated by Richard Nice. 1972. Reprint, Cambridge: Cambridge University Press, 1977.

Bradshaw, Paul F. *Eucharistic Origins*. New York: Oxford University Press, 2004.

Brown, Michael K., et al. *Whitewashing Race: The Myth of a Color-Blind Society*. Berkeley: University of California Press, 2003.

Bush, Melanie E. L. *Breaking the Code of Good Intentions: Everyday Forms of Whiteness*. Lanham, MD: Rowman & Littlefield, 2004.

Butler, Shakti. "Mirrors of Privilege: Making Whiteness Visible." Oakland: World Trust Educational Services, 2006.

Calhoun, Craig. "Habitus, Field, and Capital: The Question of Historical Specificity." In *Bourdieu: Critical Perspectives*, edited by Craig J. Calhoun et al., 61–88. Chicago: University of Chicago Press, 1993.

Calvin, John. *The Institutes of the Christian Religion*. Translated by Henry Beveridge. Grand Rapids: Eerdmans, 1989.

Carr, Leslie G. *"Color-Blind" Racism*. Thousand Oaks, CA: Sage, 1997.

Caruth, Cathy. "Introduction: Trauma and Experience." In *Trauma: Explorations in Memory*, edited by Cathy Caruth, 3–12. Baltimore: Johns Hopkins University Press, 1995.

————. *Unclaimed Experience: Trauma, Narrative, and History.* Baltimore: Johns Hopkins University Press, 1996.

Casey, Edward. "The Ghosts of Embodiment: On Bodily Habitudes and Schema." In *Body and Flesh: A Philosophical Reader,* edited by Donn Welton, 207–26. Oxford: Blackwell, 1998.

Cone, James. *The Cross and the Lynching Tree.* Maryknoll, NY: Orbis, 2011.

Connerton, Paul. *How Societies Remember.* New York: Cambridge University Press, 1989.

Copeland, M. Shawn. *Enfleshing Freedom: Body, Race, and Being.* Minneapolis: Fortress, 2010.

Dukes, E. Franklin, et al. "Collective Transitions and Community Resilience in the Face of Enduring Trauma." In *Collaborative Resilience: Moving Through Crisis to Opportunity,* edited by Bruce Evan Goldstein, 231–52. Cambridge: MIT Press, 2012.

Edwards, Korie L. *The Elusive Dream: The Power of Race in Interracial Churches.* New York: Oxford University Press, 2008.

Emerson, Michael, and Christian Smith. *Divided by Faith: Evangelical Religion and the Problem of Race in America.* New York: Oxford University Press, 2000.

Eyerman, Ron. *Cultural Trauma: Slavery and the Formation of African American Identity.* Cambridge: Cambridge University Press, 2001.

Feagin, Joe R., and Eileen O'Brien. *White Men on Race: Power, Privilege, and the Shaping of Cultural Consciousness.* Boston: Beacon, 2003.

Feagin, Joe R., and Melvin Sikes. *Living with Racism: The Black Middle-Class Experience.* Boston: Beacon, 1994.

Foley, Edward. *From Age to Age: How Christians Have Celebrated the Eucharist.* Collegeville, MN: Liturgical, 2008.

Frankenberg, Ruth, ed. *Displacing Whiteness: Essays in Social and Cultural Criticism.* Durham: Duke University Press, 1997.

Garrigan, Siobhán. *Beyond Ritual: Sacramental Theology after Habermas.* Burlington, VT: Ashgate, 2004.

Grimes, Ronald L. *Reading, Writing, and Ritualizing: Ritual in Fictive, Liturgical, and Public Places.* Washington, DC: Pastoral, 1993.

Hacker, Andrew. *Two Nations: Black and White, Separate, Hostile, Unequal.* New York: Scribner, 2003.

Haldeman, Scott. *Towards Liturgies That Reconcile: Race and Ritual among African-American and European-American Protestants.* Burlington, VT: Ashgate, 2007.

Hardin, Curtis D., and Mahzarin R. Banaji. "The Nature of Implicit Prejudice: Implications for Personal and Public Policy." In *The Behavioral Foundations of Public Policy,* edited by Eldar Shafir, 13–31. Princeton: Princeton University Press, 2012.

Harvey, Jennifer. *Dear White Christians: For Those Still Longing for Racial Reconciliation.* Grand Rapids: Eerdmans, 2014.

BIBLIOGRAPHY

Hauerwas, Stanley. *Christian Existence Today: Essays on Church, World, and Living in Between*. Durham: Labyrinth, 1988.

Keshgegian, Flora. *Redeeming Memories: A Theology of Healing and Transformation*. Nashville: Abingdon, 2000.

Kinder, Donald R., and David O. Sears. "Prejudice and Politics: Symbolic Racism versus Racial Threats to the Good Life." *Journal of Personality & Social Psychology* 40 (1981) 414–31.

Lange, Dirk. *Trauma Recalled: Liturgy, Disruption, and Theology*. Minneapolis: Fortess, 2010.

Leonard, John K., and Nathan D. Mitchell. *The Postures of the Assembly during the Eucharistic Prayer*. Chicago: Liturgy Training Publications, 1994.

Macy, Gary. *Treasures from the Storeroom: Medieval Religion and the Eucharist*. Collegeville, MN: Liturgical, 1999.

McClintock Fulkerson, Mary. *Places of Redemption: Theology for a Worldly Church*. Oxford: Oxford University Press, 2007.

McGowan, Andrew. *Ascetic Eucharists: Food and Drink in Early Christian Ritual Meals*. Oxford: Clarendon, 1999.

Metz, Johann Baptist. *Faith in History and Society: Toward a Practical Fundamental Theology*. New York: Crossroad, 2007.

———. *Love's Strategy: The Political Theology of Johann Baptist Metz*. Edited by John K. Downey. Harrisburg, PA: Trinity, 1999.

———. "Theology Today: New Crises and New Visions." In *Love's Strategy: The Political Theology of Johann Baptist Metz*, edited John K. Downey, 64–82. Harrisburg, PA: Trinity, 1999.

Miles, Sara. *Take This Bread: A Radical Conversion*. New York: Ballentine, 2007.

Mount Shoop, Marcia W. *Let the Bones Dance: Embodiment and the Body of Christ*. Louisville: Westminster John Knox, 2010.

Morrill, Bruce T. *Anamnesis as Dangerous Memory: Political and Liturgical Theology in Dialogue*. Collegeville, MN: Liturgical, 2000.

Murray, Pauli. *Pauli Murray: The Autobiography of a Black Activist, Feminist, Lawyer, Priest, and Poet*. Knoxville: University of Tennessee Press, 1989.

O'Day, Gail. "Sacraments of Friendship: Embodied Love in the Gospel of John." In *Faith and Feminism: Ecumenical Essays*, edited by B. Diane Lipsett and Phyllis Trible, 85–99. Louisville: Westminster John Knox, 2014.

Paris, Peter J. "The Theologies of Black Folk in North America: Presidential Address to the American Theological Society, March, 2012." *Theology Today* 69 (2013) 385–402.

Potapchuk, Maggie. "White Culture Handout." http://www.racialequitytools. org/resourcefiles/whtieculturehandout.pdf.

Presbyterian Church (U.S.A.). *Book of Common Worship*. Louisville: Westminster John Knox, 1993.

Public Religion Research Institute. "Americans' Racial Disconnect on Fairness and Discrimination." http://publicreligion.org/research/graphic-of-the-week/americans-racial-disconnect-on-fairness-and-discrimination/.

———. "Race and Americans' Social Networks." http://publicreligion.org/research/2014/08/analysis-social-network/.

Rambo, Shelly. *Spirit and Trauma: A Theology of Remaining.* Louisville: Westminster John Knox, 2010.

Robinson, Elaine A. *Race and Theology.* Nashville: Abingdon, 2012.

Saliers, Don E. "Liturgy and Ethics: Some New Beginnings." In *Liturgy and the Moral Self: Humanity at Full Stretch before God; Essays in Honor of Don E. Saliers,* edited by E. Byron Anderson and Bruce T. Morrill, 15–37. Collegeville, MN: Liturgical, 1998.

Saunders, Stanley P., and Charles L. Campbell. *Word on the Street: Performing the Scriptures in the Urban Context.* Grand Rapids: Eerdmans, 2000.

Scott, Margaret. *The Eucharist and Social Justice.* New York: Paulist, 2009.

Shelton, Jason E., and Michael O. Emerson. *Blacks and Whites in Christian America: How Racial Discrimination Shapes Religious Convictions.* New York: New York University Press, 2012.

Shelton, J. Nicole, et al. "Biases in Interracial Interactions: Implications for Social Policy." In *The Behavioral Foundations of Public Policy,* edited by Eldar Shafir, 32–51. Princeton: Princeton University Press, 2013.

Smith, Andrea. "First Nation, Empire, and Globalization." In *The Oxford Handbook of Feminist Theology,* edited by Mary McClintock Fulkerson and Sheila Briggs, 307–31. Oxford: Oxford University Press, 2012.

Sullivan, Shannon. *Good White People: The Problem with Middle-Class White Anti-Racism.* Albany: State University of New York Press, 2014.

Tillich, Paul. *Systematic Theology.* Vol. 2. Chicago: University of Chicago, 1957.

Van der Kolk, Bessel A., and Onno van der Hart. "The Intrusive Past: The Flexibility of Memory and the Engraving of Trauma." In *Trauma: Explorations in Memory,* edited by Cathy Caruth, 158–82. Baltimore: Johns Hopkins University Press, 1995.

Wannenwetsch, Bernd. *Political Worship: Ethics for Christian Citizens.* Translated by Margaret Kohl. Oxford: Oxford University Press, 2004.

Williams, Raymond. *Culture and Materialism: Selected Essays.* London: Verso, 2005.

———. *Culture and Society, 1780–1950.* 1958. Reprint, Nottingham: Spokesman, 2013.

———. *Keywords: A Vocabulary of Culture and Society.* Rev. ed. New York: Oxford University Press, 1983.

Wilmore, Gayraud S. *Black and Presbyterian: The Heritage and the Hope.* Rev. ed. Louisville: Witherspoon, 1998.

Wise, Tim. *Colorblind: The Rise of Post-Racial Politics and the Retreat from Racial Equity.* San Francisco: City Lights, 2010.